3-Minute
Daily
Devotions

A 365 Devotional for Teen Guys
Written by Jesse Campbell

B&H
PUBLISHING GROUP
Nashville, Tennessee

INTRODUCTION

I'm Jesse Campbell. I live in Nashville with my bride, our rambunctious boys, and our sweet little girl. In addition to writing books, I am a teaching pastor and was a professional drummer. My drumming days gave me some great stories to share with you along our way!

These 365 devotionals come straight out of the Bible and apply directly to the life of a young man such as yourself. We'll work our way through a few books at a time, in order, with a few "curveball" passages coming in from all over the Bible. I know that sometimes you need to zoom in on a specific topic, so feel free to use the subject guide located in the back of the book. (The numbers listed are based on the devotion day, not the page number.)

The experience goes beyond the book itself to jessethecampbell. com. On the BOOKS page, I've developed and uploaded material, like original songs and coaching videos, just for you. There you can also connect with other strong young men of God who are reading this book and connect with me as I share new material.

This book will challenge you specifically. It will make you uncomfortable. It will hold you accountable (as much as a book can) to evangelizing your friends and loving your enemies. You will be called to evangelize again and again. You will pray and help out as those whom you have evangelized evangelize. You will encourage fallen Christians. You will stand up on a table. You will do wild things. You will fast. You will write a letter to yourself and read it a year later. Then, you will be challenged to evangelize even your enemies and audaciously do your part to grow the kingdom of God. The world needs strong young men of God.

In Jesus' name, may you finish this book a strong—and then stronger—young man of God. Amen.

Now, WRITE A LETTER TO YOUR FUTURE SELF, seal it, and put it where you'll know where it is. Write down the letter's location in the blank below. I'll tell you when to retrieve it, long after you've forgotten it. In this letter, write a description of the strong man of God you hope to become by the time you have finished this book.

My letter to myself at this devotional's end is located:

_____

PRAYING FOR THESE:

Over the next 365 days, you will be in prayer for certain people in your life who affect or who may be affected by your walk of faith. Read the descriptions and list those people below.

Andrew and Philip were two men who were introduced to Jesus by John the Baptist, and their lives were changed forever. So was the world. Who are the Andrew and Philip in your life? (These are two other young men with whom you are going to share your faith.)

My Andrew: _____

My Philip:_____

The Pharisees were Jesus' biggest human opposition. They mocked, questioned, and discouraged Him. They, along with a counsel called the Sanhedrin, led by the high priest, Caiaphas, would eventually set the crucifixion into motion by bribing Judas. Who are the Pharisees in your life, that you may pray for them?

My Pharisees:_____

_____

_____

_____

Nicodemus was a Pharisee and member of the very counsel that was going after Jesus, but he began to secretly believe. It was to Nicodemus that Jesus spoke the words recorded in John 3:16. When this book prompts you, or whenever God lays this person on your heart, write the name of a Christian who is being secretive about his faith and trying to keep things under wraps by pretending he's not a Christian.

My Nicodemus: _____

The ultimate goal each year as you go through this devotional will be not only to see your Andrew and Philip come to Christ, be baptized, and grow in the Lord alongside you at church, but also to see one of them (in the Bible, it's Andrew) introduce someone else to Jesus. That person is Peter. Peter goes on to become a leader among the disciples, an evangelizing hero on the day of Pentecost in Acts 2, and a legend in church history. Who have you seen your Andrew and/or Philip lead to Christ?

Peter: _____

DAY 1

2 SAMUEL 23:20–23

I would like to introduce you to my second favorite person in the Bible. (My favorite is Jesus.) His name is Benaiah, and all we really know about him is that he went into a pit on a snowy day and killed a lion for some reason. Brace yourself! This is one of those Bible passages that is pretty graphic but also pretty cool. *Read today's Scripture.*

King David was a man after God's own heart, and he chose Benaiah as one of his mighty men—his own bodyguard. Benaiah's fierce strength and fearless heart were a big part of why he was chosen for this role. I know that you are likely surrounded by messages that ask you to tone down your strength and compromise some of that which makes you a man. I know the embarrassing way you see men portrayed on TV and in commercials. Listen to me: do not apologize for your wild strength. Godly men must seek after God and be fierce at times. So, do not put out the fire that God has ignited within your heart. Remember Benaiah and the way he dedicated his strength to God's cause. Do likewise, mighty man of God.

DAY 2

2 TIMOTHY 2:22

Our culture's notion of adolescence extending through a man's twenties and even into his thirties is a relatively new development in anthropological history. The young men of generations past would be appalled at the thirty-nine-year-old sitting up in his race-car bed, wearing his adult-size Star Wars pajamas, and calling out to his mommy to bring him more Oreos. They would be shocked at how common this kind of thing (well, not this kind of thing exactly) is in our culture today. In the first century, the leader of one of the largest and most important churches in the world was a young man about your age named Timothy. This is Paul's letter to him, and its words, like all the words of the Bible, apply to you and me as well. *Read today's verse*.

Flee, *flee* from pornography, laziness, and other desires that commonly ensnare young men. Instead out of a pure heart, call upon God, and do so right now. Make the proclamation to God that you are stepping up the way Timothy did. If God used someone Timothy's age back then, He can use one today.

DAY 3

AMOS 5:21–24

Today, we read the bold and confrontational words of a small-town country boy who had no education but was called by God to bring a scathing prophecy to Israel. *Read today's Scripture.*

The people of Israel were going through the motions of worship and then flagrantly neglecting the poor and needy people around them. They brought offerings out of obligation instead of gratitude. Have you ever done that? They prayed memorized prayers, like the *Shemah* and the *Selihot,* without actually *meaning* what they prayed. Have you ever mindlessly sung along with a worship song while thinking about bacon cheeseburgers or sped your way through a memorized prayer for the thousandth time? These are the same crimes against worship the Israelites committed, and Amos's harsh words spoken on behalf of Yahweh apply to *us* when we don't engage our hearts in prayer, worship, and giving!

As you close your devotional, I want you to begin what will be a new practice in your prayer, worship, and giving life. I want you to ditch those habit phrases that pop up in our prayers sometimes ("Lord, I just . . ." , etc.) and slowly think on each word. Then, let your faith flow like a stream (verse 24).

DAY 4

HEBREWS 11:32–40

Speaking of faith, scan down this chapter starting from verse 1 and pick up on this chapter's pattern before you *read today's Scripture.* It's pretty gruesome!

This chapter is called the "Hall of Faith" because it lists these heroes of the faith. *By faith* they all obeyed God's commands even when it didn't make sense and even though they would *not* be rewarded for it in their life on earth! I suppose that's partly *why* it was such great faith.

According to verse 35, some crazy strong men of God counted it an honor to suffer for Christ and actually *refused* to be released after being tortured. God is not ashamed to be called their God (verse 16), but I wonder how He feels when Christians refuse to suffer at all for their faith.

By faith, be willing to suffer for Christ. That for which you are most willing to suffer is lord in your life. May it be Jesus, and may your name be found worthy of such company as these heroes. Let it be said that you lived your life *by faith,* because without faith, it is impossible to please God (verse 6).

DAY 5

DANIEL 10:2–14

*R*ead today's Scripture. God's angel army is *powerful*. It's a jarring reality, but we are surrounded by a spiritual war, and that war affects the timing from our perspective of how some prayers are answered. This angel shot straight out of the gates of heaven the moment Daniel prayed to God but was held up for three weeks in battle with one of the most powerful demons in Satan's army (verses 12–13). This demon is called the prince of the kingdom of Persia, and he and his gang were so powerful that Daniel's messenger angel needed to call in the big guns: the archangel Michael!

Now, this angel to whom Daniel speaks—this metaphysical being whose arrival horrified Daniel's friends, whose body was like topaz, whose face was like *lightning* (whatever that means), whose eyes were like flaming torches, whose limbs were like the gleam of bronze (not like bronze; they were like the *gleam*), whose voice was like a multitude—is just a "lowly" *messenger* in the angel army! Get this: there are *twice* as many of these awesome angels as there are demons (Revelation 12:4)! Worship with Chris Tomlin's song "Whom Shall I Fear? (God of Angel Armies)" and be strengthened in faith today!

DAY 6

ISAIAH 6:1–8

*R*ead today's Scripture. These seraphim are *insanely* powerful six-winged angels. They are likely the same massive angels described in Revelation 4:8 who *never* stop praising God, saying, "Holy, holy, holy, Lord God, the Almighty." The word *holy* means to be set apart and above everything else, and to say it three times is to say it in the superlative, meaning it is the highest way to say it. So, these powerful angels *constantly* give God this highest compliment in the highest way possible. We know from Satan's fall that these angels have the freedom to do otherwise, so think on what it indicates about God's glory that these seraphim choose to spend every moment of eternity praising Yahweh in the superlative of the superlative. Whoa.

The prophet Isaiah saw the direct presence of our perfect Judge. His response was brokenness (verse 5). Brokenness can be painful. The coal is pressed to his lips, and he feels the pain that comes with awareness of one's sin in the presence of God. This sacred encounter ends with God asking whom He should send to bring God's truth to the world. Let Isaiah's answer be your own. "Here I am. Send me."

Day 7

Zephaniah 3:17

I used to struggle with the idea that God truly loved me. When I tried to imagine how God perceived me, I thought He just tolerated me most of the time and was irritated the rest. This passage showed me how outright unbiblical that thought was. It also shows that *our God is a warrior! Read today's verse.*

First off, it says that God is right there with you. He is the Warrior King of the universe, who stepped down to glorify Himself and *save* you in the process. He rejoices over you. As you run for the touchdown, He is cheering. When you are defeated, He brings you comfort in His Holy Spirit. Everything about you was deliberate. Your love for music—He gave you that. Your ability to run was His idea. He set out to create a specific man, and you are the result. *He delights* in you with shouts of joy according to this text! Just picture God shouting for joy as you become the man He created you to be.

Sing "He Will Rejoice" by Trevor Morgan on the *Glory Revealed* album. Its lyrics are straight-up *this* verse!

DAY 8

EXODUS 33:11
(Joshua and Moses: Identifying Your Male Mentor)

I know what's on your heart. I know that the heart of every man needs to be affirmed, to know that he is a man and to know it because other men see you as a man. As much as Momma loves you, this is something she cannot give. That can be a terrible source of frustration for young men whose dads either aren't around or feel as though they can't give their sons the affirmation they never received themselves. However, this is one of the beautiful purposes of the church: the ministry of masculine affirmation is something that your heavenly Father can perform as well. *Read today's verse.*

We are going to look at some of the highlights between Moses, the original leader of the Israelites, and his protégé Joshua. Here, I think that Joshua stays in the tent because his mind is blown by watching Moses talk to God *face-to-face.* He wanted what Moses had. This should be the kind of respect you have for your mentor. This is the affirmation you need. If he's not immediately obvious to you, prayerfully consider the men in your life who have enviable faiths and search for your mentor now.

DAY 9

EXODUS 17:8–16

I hope that you are never caught up in an actual battle to the death the way that Joshua is in today's text, but I do hope that you go into battle in some sense with your mentor as your ally. *Read today's text.*

As you step into your father's world, into the realm of men, you do step into a battle of sorts. You must compete. You must be willing to confront. You must be strong, and at times be the stronger. You need your own Moses who has his hands lifted toward heaven on your behalf. Not writing figuratively, I want you to know that I literally, physically just had my hands raised toward heaven on your behalf, my reader. I prayed that God, who exists outside of time, would go before me to meet you where you are as you read this, that He would give you victory. You are not alone, man. Even if no one else does, know that I have prayed for you the way that Moses prayed for Joshua. *Yes, you.*

Now, go fight the Amalekites. You are a man.

DAY 10

NUMBERS 14:1–9

Have you been let down by your hero and watched your hero fall? Don't be too hard on him, but also don't let his failures hold you back. Take his hard lesson the easy way. You'll be let down and possibly wounded by your mentor. He is not perfect, but this is no reflection of God or of you. Rather, it is an opportunity. *Read today's Scripture*.

Joshua stepped up majorly where Moses fell. Moses and Aaron are on their faces in front of the stupid back-to-Egypt committee, the wicked people of weak faith. What a disgrace! Moses, you are the *leader* of these people, and (most interpretations maintain) *they* are in the wrong! I hope you don't have to see your own Moses fall, but if you do, may you do what Joshua did, and that is courageously stand up and be stubborn about what God clearly stated as true. I hope that you have a Caleb of your own as well. Speaking of which, have you followed through with those attempts to surround yourself with wise people?

Moses will let you down, but that does not give you license to slip back: it gives you opportunity to step up.

DAY 11

NUMBERS 27:15–23

I'll never forget the time my dad first taught me to drive the tractor and use the bush hog. This tractor was one ferocious old piece of haphazard destructive force on gargantuan (seriously: more than four feet tall) tires with massive treads. The bush hog is basically a shallow, rickety, open metal chamber that follows behind the tractor and spins these enormous blades at tornado-wind speeds. My dad's invitation for me to operate this beast was affirming in itself. He showed me the basics and then went inside to drink some sweet tea. I love that he did that, just trusted me to handle it. The fact that he *commissioned* me proved that he believed in me. *Read today's passage.*

I pray that you have your own Numbers 27 affirmation experience. It proves you have what it takes, and it heals the wound on your heart. If there is no father figure in your life to affirm you this way, then get this: in Matthew 28:18–20, Jesus *commissioned* you! He trusted you with the most important task in the universe and then went to heaven . . . possibly to drink some sweet tea.

My student, you *must* be a man because you have been commissioned and therefore affirmed by God.

DAY 12

1 CORINTHIANS 16:13

Yes, you do have what it takes to be a man. Yes. That you are reading this and have read this far proves that. I know that your heart aches to know it, and these words are likely read only by those who do. Whether your dad is around or not, whether he says it to you or not, God has given you what you need to be a man. Know that you are a man. *Read today's text*.

This was the final exhortation in Paul's first letter to the church of Corinth. Prove to yourself that you have what it takes by standing by your Christian faith and doing everything you do with great amounts of love. Today, you will act like the Ultimate Man, and that is Jesus. Today, sacrifice your own interests, well-being, time, even safety, if necessary for someone else. This is what men are called to do. You *do* have what it takes to act like a man. Now, prove it today by living out this scriptural exhortation through self-sacrifice: the ultimate masculine action.

DAY 13

MALACHI 3:8–10

Today's text is unique. It's about money and tithing (giving one tenth of your income to your church or some ministry), but it's also an insanely rare instance in which God actually says to us, "Test Me. . . ." It's about to get old-school, y'all. *Read today's text.*

We are so blessed to be able to tithe—to worship by giving back to the God who gives. My wife and I love it. The offering is our favorite part of worship. It's just so fulfilling to give even a small gift to God because our hearts are so intensely grateful for all that God has given us. This text shows that it's all God's anyway because refusing or failing to tithe is robbing God! Read verse 10 one more time and resolve that you will not only bring a tithe to worship this week, but also offer something above and beyond that. My student, I promise you: a tithing lifestyle and generous heart are richly rewarded by God. Tithe, young man, out of a worshipful and grateful heart so that you will be blessed both in the act of giving and in the fulfillment of Malachi 3:10 in your life.

DAY 14

PSALM 51:1–9

What happens after you've been busted in sin? What happens when you've completely blown it spiritually in a big way? How do you pray to a holy and perfect God, who judges the universe, after that? You pray the way that David did here in Psalm 51 after cheating on his wife with Bathsheba; murdering Bathsheba's husband, Uriah; and lying to cover it all up. Let this whole psalm be the passionate prayer of your heart after you've fallen deep into sin. *Read today's text.*

In the first half of this passage, take note of how authentic David is before God in confessing his sin: he doesn't try to cover it up, he doesn't make excuses, he doesn't pass blame, and he doesn't try to polish his sin to make it look like it's not so bad. *He owns it and gets real before God* (verses 3–6). So, in confessing his sin before God (1 John 1:9), he throws himself on the victorious grace, faithful love, and abundant compassion of God (verse 1). God already knows about your sin, so it only makes sense to be real before Him about it right now.

DAY 15

PSALM 51:10–17

This is the most beautiful prayer of repentance ever written. It was prayed by a busted adulterer and murderer, but I have seen people actually borrow language from it when they pray to God as they are saved. I cannot tell you how many times I have prayed this psalm out to God. Memorize this! *Read today's passage.*

So, what was the result of this prayer? God actually restored David, continued to bless him anyway (which is utterly incredible, by the way), and David to this day is revered as the best king Israel ever had. In fact, the Star of David is at the center of Israel's national flag today. Ask God to create a new heart in you, to restore the joy of your salvation, and to give you a steadfast and willing spirit (verses 10–12). God is always compassionate to those who come to Him in a broken state, those who are deeply sorry for their sin (verse 17). Let this be your prayer after getting caught up in pornography and any kind of lust. It worked for the first guy who prayed it, and it will work for you if you pray it genuinely.

DAY 16

PSALM 51:18–19

So, after owning his sin completely (Psalm 51:1–9) and asking God to be restored fully, David is about to respond in worship gratefully. It can feel awkward to follow the sin of lust with worship. It can feel as if you don't deserve to worship God, but the funny thing is that we don't deserve God's presence even at our best moments. There is no better thing to do right after hitting rock bottom with the sin of lust than to just abIde in the grace of God. *Read today's Scripture.*

So, here is the final application of David's prayer of repentance. He committed in verse 13 to teach other people what he learned from his prodigal experience, and in verse 19 he commits to bring a massive offering in worship to God, saying that whole bulls will be put on the altar! That's just how people got their worship on in the Old Testament. These days, that means to get your tail to a place where you can worship your guts out and give God your absolute best offering of praise because you have been spared what you deserve for your sin!

DAY 17

ISAIAH 40:28–31

Today, I want you to be restored by these awe-inspiring words of hope. *Read today's text.*

Discouraged and fallen young man, don't you know who your God is? Don't you know that Yahweh is the everlasting Creator God, who never gets tired or confused or shocked? Get strength from Him right now. Let these words pour over you and fill in the cracks of your heart as they do. Did you read verse 30? That one was about you, but get this: if you trust in the Lord right now, your strength will be renewed. You may be walking now, but you will soon run and, after that, even soar on wings like an eagle!

Remember who your God is today, and let that fill you with immeasurable strength. Soar.

DAY 18

ROMANS 10:9

Here is the sequence of verses I use to evangelize. I have them marked and highlighted in my Bible so that I can share them directly with someone by just sliding the Bible across the table and letting him literally take God's Word for it.

- John 3:16—God loves you and has a plan for your life.
- Romans 3:23—Even good people are sinners.
- Romans 6:23—The consequences for that sin is death.
- John 14:6—It is Jesus Himself who says that He is the only way to be saved.
- Romans 10:9—If you confess that Jesus is Lord (meaning He's the boss and you're not) and believe with all of your heart that He rose again from the grave after being crucified for your sins, you will be saved.

Mark these passages in order and highlight them so that your Bible is battle ready. Once you've laid this out there, *give Philip and/or Andrew the chance to respond* by praying these Scriptures out to God.

DAY 19

MATTHEW 28:18–20

I want you to memorize this passage because, though all Scripture is important, this passage is especially important. It is Jesus' final big command, and it's so important, it even has a name. It's called the "Great Commission." *Read today's Scripture.*

It's rare that Jesus would throw His weight around before issuing a command this way. He delivers this commissioning (a sending-out) with *all* the authority of heaven and earth. Argue with that! This command overrides the laws of men. This is why we break the laws of anti-Christian nations to do mission work. It is an explicit statement of the will of God, and it's to go to *all* nations, to make disciples, to baptize them, and to teach them everything including this Great Commission. So, the cycle of Christianity begins and the process is not complete until new believers are commissioned. This is the big payoff for our disciples whom we met at the beginning! They were dropouts who are now promoted to rabbis! This is why I want you to see your Philip and Andrew bring a third party, whom we're calling Peter, to Christ. The process is not complete until the evangelized evangelizes! Don't give up! *Go!*

DAY 20

ROMANS 12:17–21

Bullies. Like zits in the mirror, we all face them at some point. *Read today's text.*

Yes, you could physically defend yourself, and there is absolutely a time to be strong and courageous like Joshua. However, you could give your bully a big black eye and mess up spiritually. Read verse 18 again. *If* it is possible to be cool with everyone, do it, but this verse also acknowledges that there is only so much you can do. When it's impossible to keep the peace, try to do as verse 19 says, and turn your injustices over to God. You'll be amazed at how He will step in and handle things.

Of course, when dealing with bullies, physical safety is a priority. Make sure that the people in charge know what's going on, be prepared to defend yourself, and keep your testimony intact. Bullies are usually acting out because they are hurting, and your enemy can use these guys to tempt you to publicly blow your witness. Shouting profanity and initiating violence is not conquering your bully: it is being conquered by evil. Taking the abuse to heart and letting it eat you alive also allows evil to get the best of you. Try to understand the root of the bully's anger, and heap fiery coals on his head (verse 20) by conquering evil with good (verse 21).

DAY 21

RUTH 1:1–17

(Ready . . . and . . . NEW SERIES! BABAM!)

Ruth is my favorite book of the Bible because it parallels the love story of my wife and me. My being inspired by the book of Ruth, combined with really cool interventions by the sovereignty of God, made for a *beautiful* dating relationship and eventual marriage. I want you to be like the guy in this story named Boaz. That name is just about manlier than A.1. sauce on a flaming mountain of beards.

Before you start, you need to know the Hebrew concept of *goel,* which is the practice of looking after a widow in your family either by buying your deceased brother's or male cousin's property from her or by marrying her if you're available. *Goel* is translated "family redeemer" in the CSB and "guardian-redeemer" in the NIV (Ruth 2:20). Also, know that women in this day and age did not have the rights and opportunities they deserved. So, widows with no relatives nearby—widows like Naomi, Ruth, and Orpah here—were completely without hope. Oh yeah, and there was a massive famine going on, so that's nice. *Read today's Scripture.*

Take Ruth's profession of loyalty to Naomi and make a similar profession to God right now.

Ruth 1:16–22
(Deliberate overlap)

Ruth's profession of loyalty to Naomi was bigger than one hopeless widow clinging to another. It transcended and defied incredible racial, political tension between Ruth's people, the Moabites, and Naomi's people, the Israelites. Though Moab was a tiny country, God would use it to kick the tail of His mighty chosen Israel as an act of discipline. Imagine the state of Rhode Island sometimes randomly just conquering every other state in the United States. People wouldn't like Rhode Islanders very much. For the same reason, Israelites couldn't stand Moabites. Now read Ruth's proclamation again, knowing that she is completely leaving her people behind to go to a people group who likely would have hated her. *Read today's Scripture.*

Naomi has good reason to be devastated, but there is never good reason to be bitter toward our Savior God. Take a minute and give yourself a gut check. Do you harbor any bitterness toward God? Remember, even in our suffering, God is bringing about something beautiful. It may not seem like it now, but God is bringing about His most amazing miracle ever through this little story. This will not be the last time God provides for the famine-stricken world in the city of Bethlehem.

DAY 23

RUTH 2:1-3

What seems completely random is often in the center of what God intended. This happens often in Ruth. An ancient, obscure law requiring harvesters to leave their leftovers for foreigners, widows, and orphans will play a massively important role in God's greatest miracle. *Read today's passage.*

Like Ruth, my wife had recently had her heart broken, and because of her missionary work, she was a stranger in a strange land. Meanwhile, I was on my way out of a crushing heartbreak, and through a "random" invitation from an old friend, was on my way to Chick-fil-A. Similarly, Ruth "just so happens" to be in the portion of land belonging to one of two people in the whole country who could help her and Naomi. Look at the way Ruth is handling her grief and devastation: she is getting out there and taking what she can of the harvest. Look at Naomi: sitting at home and telling people to call her "bitter." Little do they know, in the midst of their heartbreak, God is moving to bring about something amazing. So, get up from your heartbreak, dude. God is working on something you may not yet be able to understand.

DAY 24

RUTH 2:4–12

Speaking of being a generous man, look at the way Boaz gives and gives and gives. He's an admired and respected man of upright character. He speaks blessings over his employees, and they bless him right back. Wow. If his employees love him, he must be legit. *Read today's Scripture.*

Be like Boaz. The dude gives both monetarily and through encouraging words. In these few verses, he speaks three blessings over others. Look at how protective he is over Ruth. Had she gathered in someone else's field, she may have been put in danger. Boaz protects her. Be a protector of women.

Today is Boaz Day. You are to open doors for women, pull out chairs for them, let them go before you in line, and in general be a generous protector like Boaz. Encourage people, pay for someone's lunch, and speak Scripture to someone the way Boaz does to Ruth in verse 12. Today, on Boaz Day, you will find yourself more blessed than anyone. Today, on Boaz Day, you learn about being a husband and a giving man of God. Happy Boaz Day. I'll bet you won't give more than me. Bring it!

DAY 25

RUTH 2:13–19

Read today's Scripture. Boaz sent Ruth back home with twenty-six quarts of barley! That's like one of those big pallets of Honey Bunches of Oats! She took it home, and Naomi was massively impressed. She was grateful that Boaz both protected and honored Ruth. It's so important to have the mom's blessing and for her to know that you are a man of God and a man of purity.

When my wife and I were dating, I protected our purity by never letting us find ourselves alone together in a house. Extreme? No: *effective.* As a result, we spent a lot of time getting coffee. One day, after three coffee trips and no surf, we went to a park and chilled in the grass until we fell asleep. I woke up a while later to see that my wife had ditched me to sleep in the car, and that very moment her mom was passing by on a walk with her friend in that park after work! She introduced her friend to the apparently homeless man with grass in his hair who was dating her daughter. It was funny, but more importantly it proved to my future mother-in-law that we were pure.

DAY 26

RUTH 2:20–23

Read today's passage. There is no way it was just a coincidence that Ruth gleaned in Boaz's field of all the fields in Judah. Ruth was just getting up and getting out there, and God was guiding her as she did. God is doing something enormous through the little details of this story, and it will all come into focus soon. Ruth "happened" to be in the field belonging to one of her and Naomi's family redeemers, someone related to Naomi's dead husband who could save them from abject poverty.

This is a turning point for Naomi. She has been stuck in her negativity and bitterness until this moment. I'll bet she felt convicted to know that as she sat at home on her keister, being bitter and angry toward God, He was in the process of bringing about her redemption. Get real with yourself right now and see if you're being like Naomi in the face of your trial and difficulty. If so, you are missing the chance to say you never lost faith when things were tough. You're being like Thomas and blowing an opportunity to demonstrate faith.

DAY 27

RUTH 3:1–11

Read today's passage. As I was working on my paper about Ruth, I knew God was telling me that it was proposal time. My wife and I had dated with the purpose of figuring out whether or not we were supposed to be married and had protected our purity. I had some proposal ideas, including proposing on a roller coaster, and secretly had been working on a reggae-style song for her. So, I went to the jewelry store completely unaware it would be the one day out of the year . . . that diamonds were on sale.

The way Ruth wakes Boaz up is insanely similar to the way my wife woke me up from a nap . . . the day I was planning to propose to her. If this wasn't enough, my mom called me as I looked down on Jessi lying at the base of the couch with my blanket's corner over her and said, "Jesse, I had this dream that you sang some reggae-type song to Jessi and ended it with the words, 'Jessi, will you marry me?'" My mind was blown. We were in Ruth 3!

Take notes from Boaz here as you find your Ruth. God is in control.

DAY 28

RUTH 3:12–18

I'm writing this devotional from thirty-six thousand feet in the air. That has nothing to do with today's text. I just wanted to share it. *Read today's text.*

Ruth, in following Naomi's advice, does a great job at making it known to Boaz that she is available and interested. She leaves the rest to Boaz, who is stoked about the idea, but there is one problem: he is not the most closely related person to Naomi's dead husband. He could have left this out. He could have glossed over this fact, but he addresses it. He has integrity and sticks by the truth even when it threatens what he wants. Do likewise.

Also, I want you to treat the women in your life with the kind of careful wisdom that Boaz demonstrates as he plans out his every move to protect Ruth's reputation. He wanted her to be respected. Let the reputations of the young women in your life be protected and elevated because of their association with you. Do everything in a way that is aboveboard and honorable.

DAY 29

RUTH 4:1–12

Boaz is about to take care of business like a boss . . . like a Hebrew boss. People didn't have phones, so he's going to wait where he's sure to catch the man who was first in line according to *goel* custom to marry Ruth. Then, his plan is to bring him to the nearby assembly of elders. These elders were the respected older men of the town who governed and made big decisions like this one. After that, it gets a little weird from our perspective as they trade sandals to seal the deal, but just imagine what men of that era would think of our handshake. "So, you guys hold hands . . . and then move them up and down? That's weird." *Read today's Scripture.*

Swoosh. Everything goes according to Boaz's plan. He gets the girl! Now, take note of his confidence. He knows what he wants, and he has a plan to get it. Boaz risked his future with Ruth when he could have just slipped under the radar and proposed to her! This causes other men, including the elders, to respect him greatly. He is absolutely transparent and straightforward. Conduct yourself like Boaz today. Conduct yourself like a man.

Day 30

Ruth 4:13–22 and Matthew 1:5–6, 16

*R*ead *Ruth 4:13–22.* So, this story of two grief-stricken, impoverished, hungry widows ends in complete restoration! Naomi has gone from a deep, dark, and bitter depression to optimism to such joy that even those who see her story unfold become believers and spread the truth of God (verse 14). Ruth's incredible declaration of faithfulness in the beginning seemed so foolish at first, but has more than paid off, and Boaz has a bride and a son. Talk about redemption! But there is so much *more*.

Read Matthew 1:5–6, 16. The story just rushed from Ruth to King David to Christ to your face, right where you sit, stand, or lie. All along, we were reading the genealogy of Jesus Christ the Son of God. As Ruth and Naomi wept for their dead first husbands, clutching their burning empty stomachs, and walking north out of Moab to cross the Jordan River, wondering where God was in their tragedy, God was bringing about the ultimate miracle of all time: the line of David including Solomon and ultimately salvation for all who would believe in Ruth's descendant Jesus. God is working in your hardships!

Day 31

John 1:1–18

Who are you? Seriously, answer the question. If you don't have an identity, then the world is happy to shape your identity for you. Turn your TV on and find a comedy. I'll bet you my . . . neighbor's cat that most of the male characters you see are dumber than a wet sack of aardvarks, and they desperately need to be cared for by the women on the show. That's not you. With the Holy Spirit dwelling within you, you can become the man you were designed by God to be, the man the world desperately needs right now: a strong man of God. Together, we can find the affirmation for which every young man so desperately longs. *Read today's Scripture.*

The Bible right in front of you once walked this earth in the flesh of a man, and His name is Jesus. He is the ultimate example for us as men because He performed the greatest act of masculinity: self-sacrifice. Together, we will do likewise. Like Jesus, your Bible gives perfect wisdom. According to verse 12, you have been given the right to call yourself God's. That is who you are. That is whose you are.

DAY 32

JOHN 1:19–34

Read today's Scripture. I want you to strive to be like John the Baptist today. I want you to be like this guy whom Matthew 3:4 describes as a little crazy. He wore camel's hair bound by a massive belt and ate locusts along with something the Bible calls "wild honey," which I can only assume means he ate some bees along with the honey straight out of the hive. Yes, this unkempt wild man is the one I want you to emulate—not so much in that I want you to stop bathing, but that you should, as he does in today's text, stand up to the Pharisees because he knows exactly who he is. Later on, he also boldly states outright that Jesus is God. Do likewise today, locust eater.

DAY 33

JOHN 1:35–51

Did you stand up to the Pharisees, like John the Baptist yesterday? Who are the Pharisees in your life: those people who would question why you do what God made you to do, try to influence you away from it, and mock you as you go for it? Consider who your Pharisees are and write their names on the "Praying for These" page next to the "My Pharisees" line.

Now, *read today's Scripture*. John the Baptist pointed these men toward Jesus, and as a result the history of our planet was forever altered. You can also be a part of changing someone's world just by introducing him to Jesus the way John the Baptist did. Today, being like the wild man John the Baptist, you will point lost people toward Jesus, even by doing nothing more than inviting someone to church with you. Go get 'em, wild man!

DAY 34

PROVERBS 1:1–33

Pray now for your Pharisees; then pray for those you pointed toward Jesus yesterday. Lift them up to God and pray that they would become aware of God's love for them this very instant, making note of the time as you do. When you see them, ask them about their morning (or whatever time you prayed for them). Write their names on the "Praying for These" page next to "My Andrew" and "My Phillip." The line for "Peter," we will save for later.

Read today's Scripture.

A strong man of God has wisdom, and the beginning of wisdom is knowing God. This book was written by Solomon, who, before he became a huge creep (we can get into that later), was offered anything he wanted from God. He chose wisdom, and with that wisdom, he wrote the book of Proverbs as well as some other great stuff in the Bible. Today, we come to feel the weight of wisdom, appreciate how valuable it is, and aspire to have it no matter what. The main way you are going to get the wisdom of a strong man of God is by diving deep into God's Word!

DAY 35

PROVERBS 2:1–15

Read today's Scripture. Crave wisdom, young man. Crave it so ferociously that your jaw clenches, your hands become fists, and your nostrils flare as you think about how bad you want it. If you live on the bottom floor of your house or apartment, I literally want you to get on your knees right now and pound the floor with your fist as you cry out to God, "I NEED GODLY WISDOM!"

Did you do it? I was serious. Do it now if you haven't.

Most young men live their lives according to what their flesh tells them they want, but not you. Most of your friends are susceptible to the lies of the crooked men described in verses 12–15, but not you. Most young guys are lust-driven machines, but today that is not you.

Just for fun, pound the floor one more time. Tell them I told you to do it.

DAY 36

PROVERBS 2:16-22

Read today's Scripture. Yep, this is one of those books—one of those books that talks about lust. The wisdom of a strong man of God helps him to see how dangerous lust is in all of its forms. A godly man with godly wisdom has just as much of a sex drive as his counterparts, who are lusting after anything with a pulse. The difference is, a man with godly wisdom shows self-control because he is filled with the Holy Spirit (Galatians 5 and Romans 8), and he has his eyes fixed on the end zone: marriage.

Today, because you are developing the wisdom of a strong man of God, you will not be led astray by girls like the one described in verse 16. Let the other dogs fight over their kibbles and bits; you are much too wise for that. You're holding out for a much greater prize. You are waiting on your steak.

Also, have you been journaling? If not, you're robbing yourself of a future blessing!

DAY 37

PSALM 34:15–22

Today, we're going to break from working our way through Proverbs to talk about another important topic. (We'll do this occasionally.) Let's talk about how to deal with a broken heart. When I was in high school, I dated a girl for two and a half years. It ended when I found out that she kissed this other guy. I was crushed! I still remember the pain. After a few days in an epic slump, these verses brought me roaring back to life. It's this beautiful psalm of David about deliverance that doubles as a prophecy about Jesus' crucifixion. Get this: it was written hundreds of years before crucifixion really existed. *Read today's Scripture*.

God's eyes and ears are on you right now. He is near and *He saves those who are crushed in spirit*. You take refuge in Him. Give Him all of your pain, because He cares for you.

DAY 38

JAMES 1:1–4

John is a Gospel, Proverbs a book of wisdom, and James an "epistle." It was written by the half brother of Jesus (half because Jesus' Father is God), James, who was the leader of the church in Jerusalem. Jesus' earthly brothers at first did not believe that Jesus was who He said He was. As you can understand, your brothers would probably be the hardest people on the planet to convince that you are actually God. So, the fact that James not only came to believe that his brother was God, but also became a church leader and even gave his life telling *others* that Jesus was God is historically verifiable proof of God. *Read today's Scripture.*

Our difficulties are to be considered a source of joy not because of the suffering they bring, but because of the perseverance they develop. Now, before you tune me out, there is something you should know about me: one of my sons died. His name is Aiden. Our family's trial and pain can't be described here, but I can tell you that I am joyful for the perseverance the experience gave me. I can endure anything now. So you can believe me when I say that I am not asking you to do anything I have not done myself. Be grateful for the perseverance that comes from the difficult things in your life today.

DAY 39

JAMES 1:5–8

Since we have been asking God for wisdom with our fists (I hope you haven't made enemies of any downstairs neighbors; we may want to evangelize them later), it is very important that we actually believe God will give it to us. What would be the point in praying a prayer you do not believe God will answer? What kind of man would pray in such a way? *Read today's Scripture.*

A double-minded and unstable man—that's what kind of man. Take this teaching and press it hard against your prayer life. When you're pleading to God for wisdom, is it coming from a heart that's being real? Let's make sure right now. This time, don't stop pounding until you genuinely believe that God is able to give you the wisdom you seek. Believe in God just as much as you believe in that floor you're pounding.

DAY 40

JAMES 1:9–12

Isn't it funny how both destitute people *and* rich people think about money all the time? Those who feel that they need more money strive for it, and those who have it are either terrified of losing it or just hungry for even more. The funny thing is that, once this life is over, none of it will matter. If Jesus is your Lord, then you will one day find yourself in the perfect kingdom of heaven, where those who had tons of money on earth no longer have any need for it and those who had nothing on the earth are just as rich. *Read today's Scripture.*

Don't be too caught up in worldly things, because they ultimately won't matter (Colossians 3). Also, did you catch verse 12? God has a crown of life in store for you if you persevere through your trials. Wow! I can't wait to see what that means one day.

DAY 41

JOHN 2:1–12

Read today's Scripture. Jesus performs the first miracle of His ministry in this passage. The fact that it took place at a wedding is really cool to me. In those days, the groom funded the party, and this poor guy had run out of drinks for his party guests. This was considered a bad sign of his abilities as a provider for his bride. But in steps Jesus, who fills these massive ceremonial washing jars *to the brim* with 120 to 180 gallons of wine. Wine was also heavily symbolic not only in their culture, but throughout Jesus' ministry.

Take a moment to savor how enjoyable this wedding party is because much of the rest of the Gospel of John is going to be different. More importantly, face this day knowing that when Jesus fills, He fills *to the brim*. Be filled to the brim with the Spirit of God as you walk through the halls today.

DAY 42

JOHN 2:13-25

Take a minute to visualize someone busting through the doors of your church, shouting at people, throwing tables over, smashing up stacks of money, and cracking a whip. Do you have that mental video rolling? Now, *read today's Scripture.* Whoa, that was Jesus!

There is so much to appreciate about this text, from Jesus' prophesying His coming resurrection to His fury over the injustice going on at the temple to verse 25's mind-blowing and convicting truth about Jesus knowing what is in each person. But for now, if nothing else, I just want you to walk away with a more accurate picture of Jesus in your mind. Discard those pictures of a pale, white dude in feminine-looking robes who looks like He just had a facial. Visualize the events of this passage and let that paint a portrait of Jesus for you.

Did you know that He did this *twice*? Imagine their faces when He showed up the second time. "This guy again?!"

DAY 43

JOHN 3:1–21

Pray for the Pharisees on your list, and after you have, answer this question: do you honestly believe that they could become Christians? Today we read about a Pharisee who came to believe in Jesus. *Read today's Scripture.*

Boom! There's the most famous verse in the Bible, and many don't realize that it was spoken to a Pharisee. Did you notice that Nicodemus wanted to meet Jesus at night? This is because he did not want to be found out by his fellow Pharisees. That is why Jesus used the imagery of light and darkness and why He essentially called Nicodemus to come into the light in verse 21.

Are you like Nicodemus? Are you a closet Christian? For that matter, do you truly believe in Jesus the way John 3:16 describes saving belief? In either case, may you come into the light today!

DAY 44

PROVERBS 3:1–26

Aaaaand we're back to Proverbs, where we learn about the value of godly wisdom. *Read today's Scripture.*

Let's take what is intended as a word picture and apply it literally. Verse 3 calls us to tie love and faithfulness around our necks, and verse 1 tells us not to forget God's teachings. So today, I want you to wear a necklace—not some girly necklace with a fairy on it, but something more like a velociraptor claw framed by bear teeth tied together with shark intestines. Seriously, wear some sort of cool necklace today, and every time you notice it, recite verses 5 and 6 from memory. If someone else points it out, you have to say verses 5 and 6 aloud to them. Go!

Proverbs 3:27–35

*R*ead *today's Scripture.* These verses all have to do with how we interact with those around us. Notice how verses 32–35 are structured with one half referring to godly men and the other half referring to ungodly men. This kind of verse structure is going to be all over the book of Proverbs. The upright, righteous, humble, and wise man always comes out on top, doesn't he?

The man who abides by verses 27–31 seems as though he would be a really cool guy to me because he would always treat people fairly, would never intend harm to anyone, and wouldn't accuse people who haven't wronged him. Be that guy. Chances are, you will have the chance to be that guy at some point today. Don't waste the opportunity when it arises.

Remember yesterday's teaching to not forget God's commands? (How ironic if you've already forgotten. Ha!) Today is a day for living out all of Proverbs 3.

DAY 46

PROVERBS 4:1–17

Fatherhood may seem like a far-off notion right now, but it is never too early to start preparing for fatherhood one day. The decisions you make today affect the kind of father you will be years from now.

Read today's Scripture. Here, Solomon says to his sons that he was once a son. In fact, he describes how he was still very much in the realm of his mother until his father said the words of this chapter to him and those words contrast wisdom with evil. Wow! Think about that: the opposite of wisdom is evil! It is no wonder that Solomon encourages us so vigorously to get wisdom at any cost. Also, I want you to think about this biblically described transition that is necessary for every young man: you must at some point step out of the realm of your mother's nourishing care as a tender boy and step into the world of men.

DAY 47

JAMES 1:13–20

This question may seem weird at first, but I want you to truly consider it: how do you think God views you? To some that question might be downright scary. *I'm so afraid God might view me as a nuisance,* one might think. Or, *Based on how my life has gone, I'd say God is not my biggest fan.*

Read today's Scripture. Now, ask yourself that question again, this time remembering that the words you just read were inspired directly by God. God is a giver of good and perfect gifts. Verses 19–20 give us our challenge for the day. Today, you will be slow to speak, quick to listen, and slow to become angry.

DAY 48

JAMES 1:21-25

The word *therefore* comes up a lot in Scripture. One of my professors in seminary (a post-college college for people who want to learn more about ministry) always said, "When you see a *therefore*, back up and see what it's *there for*." Brace yourself: a *therefore* is coming. You know what to do when you see it. *Read today's Scripture.*

Verse 21 is a straight-up call to *get rid* of *all* moral filth. For that matter, this whole passage is really straightforward. Don't just read the Bible. *Do* the Bible. (This is why we have a challenge in almost all of our devotions.) So, get rid of moral filth and act upon what you know about the Bible. Be brutal with the moral filth in your life today!

DAY 49

JAMES 1:26

Read today's Scripture. Harsh, huh? The language you use and so often the words you *don't* use are the most immediate giveaway as to whether or not you take your testimony as a Christian seriously. When I hear someone cuss or go off on some angry, hurtful rant in public, it's pretty safe to say that person does not particularly care to be seen as a Christian who intends to stick by God's Word. Also, when someone speaks with excessive words and just rambles, I am less likely to take him seriously. Remember: this verse is not just about profanity, but about keeping a tight rein over your tongue.

Day 50

John 3:22–36

Remember our slightly unhygienic, camel-wearing friend who made bizarre dietary choices and generally made people nervous? John the Baptist, the one whom I so desperately want you to be like, is back. *Read today's Scripture.*

When people tell him that Jesus is getting all up on his baptizing turf, John essentially says, "Awesome! That's the point!" Read verse 30 again and say it aloud right now. Mean it when you do.

Verse 36 should have a huge impact on the way we see ourselves if we are saved and the way we see others who are not saved. We who believe in Jesus were once under God's wrath, and those who do not believe in Jesus are currently headed toward wrath. Let that fill your heart with motivation to speak up John-the-Baptist style today. Remember: He must become greater, and we must become less.

DAY 51

JOHN 4:1–26

*R*ead *today's Scripture.* Women played enormous roles in Jesus' permanently world-changing ministry, and He treated them with respect and dignity during a time when women were treated terribly. This woman is not only a Samaritan (someone who believed much like a Jew, but with some differences in religious practice and ancestry), but a Samaritan *woman*—and not just a Samaritan woman, but a Samaritan woman with a bad reputation!

She is the one to whom Jesus gives the most beautiful teaching about worship in the Bible. Right now, turn on your worship music and worship God in spirit and in truth. That means for you to worship God, who is a spiritual being you cannot see, while filled with the Holy Spirit. Worship in absolute honesty. See, Jesus' prophecy in verse 21 came true right there where you are having your devotional!

DAY 52

JOHN 4:27–42

Visualize today's passage in split screen mode. The two scenes going on simultaneously in verses 27–39 are going to collide in verse 40. On one side of the screen, Jesus tells His disciples about how sharing their faith is like sowing and harvesting crops, while on the other side of the screen, the Samaritan woman from yesterday's Scripture is sharing her faith and harvesting a crop! *Read today's passage.*

Notice the way the woman shared her faith. She just told people about her encounter with Jesus, and then in verse 42, they came to know for themselves that Jesus really is the Savior of the world. Today, just tell people about how *you* came to know Jesus so that they might come to know Him as well. In doing so, you will likely be sowing seeds in their hearts, but you also just might get to be a part of the harvest today!

Day 53

Proverbs 4:18–27

*R*ead *today's Scripture.* Have you noticed how many times in the past two chapters Solomon writes about his sons' hearts? My Bible lists it six times! Did you know that if God were given the choice between your obedience to all the laws of the Bible and your heart, God would rather have your heart? You see, if God has your heart, you will want to obey His commands. This is why, in verse 23, we are encouraged to guard our hearts *above all else.* Everything we do flows from our hearts.

Also, look at the laser-like focus to which we are called as strong young men of God (verses 20–27). Today, Satan is going to try to distract you from the progress you've made. It may not even be by tempting you into sin, but by having you chase something less than God's best for you. However, you'll be ready because you're going to reread verses 25–27 *riiiiiiiiiight . . .* wait for it . . . *now.*

DAY 54

PROVERBS 5:1–14

Ninety-eight percent of young men, even godly young men, struggle with lust. The other 2 percent either pretend not to, or live on the polar ice caps. You are not alone in this. Read that last sentence again. It's true. To be *tempted* by lust, whether it's pornography or any other form, is not a sin. It becomes sin when you bite the bait with the hook in it and act upon that temptation. *Read today's Scripture.*

Verses 3–6 describe the hook hidden in the bait. The woman in a pornographic image or video does not have your best interest at heart. The girl who would tempt you to compromise your purity is inviting you down the wrong road, man. Whatever brief and short-lived fun you may find that pornography and lust bring is not at all worth the damage they will do to your walk with God, not to mention your heart toward women, including your future wife. There is a reason God put an entire chapter about lust in His book on wisdom for young men. Be wise.

DAY 55

PROVERBS 5:15–20

Because I love my wife so much and because I'm a man of God, I will never cheat on my wife. On October 18, 2008, we crossed the finish line of marriage with our virginities intact (yes, it is absolutely possible) and came to fully understand why God gave us sex drives at all. There is a purpose behind your hardwired desire and curiosity about sex: that you and your future wife would enjoy it, and in that enjoyment be a part of the means by which God creates human life! Sex is not just physical; it's spiritual too. Just as God decreed would happen in the Garden of Eden when He created marriage, my wife and I became one and are satisfied sexually in a way that God not only approves of, but actually encourages! *Read today's Scripture*—and do so with maturity.

I know that the struggle with lust is unbelievably intense right now, but it helps to know that God has a design for your sex drive. Sex is better where it was intended to be, and that is between a husband and wife.

DAY 56

JAMES 1:27

Take a minute to start this devotional off with some deep prayer for the Pharisees, Andrew, and Phillip listed on your "Praying for These" page. Think honestly now: have you lived out the Christian life with integrity before them? Have you invited them to church with you? Resolve before God to do so today, and then *read today's Scripture.*

So, the kind of religion that God respects is not one of ritual and routine, but is one that looks after orphans and widows and keeps you from being polluted by the world. Today, I want you to use the Internet for something Satan doesn't want you using it for. I want you to do some research on organizations like Compassion International and Bethany Christian Services. Then, speak with your parents about any widows who attend your church or live near you. See if there is anything you can do for them like bring them a meal or do their yard work for free. *That* is religion.

DAY 57

JAMES 2:1–13

Read today's Scripture. In James's day, people who were rich often became rich because they wickedly trumped up false charges against the poor, dragged them into court, and were favored by the judge because they were rich. You might not be suing the pants off of people who already do not have much, but you are still subject to the temptation to show favoritism.

Today, we prove to ourselves that we are actually free from favoritism by stepping out of the usual social bubble and actively choosing to be around those who are most rejected. That person who sits alone in the cafeteria, on the bus, in the corner of the gym when he is supposed to be playing basketball, or wherever he sits will not sit alone today. Instead, you are going to sit with him.

DAY 58

JAMES 2:14–26

When Abraham brought Isaac up the mountain in Genesis 22, it was out of obedience to God's inexplicable call that he sacrifice his only son, Isaac—the very son God gave to him so that an entire nation would begin through his descendants. The scene that unfolded was one big preview of the crucifixion that would take place centuries upon centuries later. Just as Abraham raised the knife to his only son on top of a mountain with an altar lined by the very wood his son carried up the hill, God would one day give His one and only Son on top of a mountain on a cross that Jesus carried most of the way Himself. Just as Abraham received his son back (Hebrews 11:19) as Isaac got up from that altar because God provided the sacrifice, Jesus the Son of God arose from the grave, and God provided the sacrifice for our sins. *Read today's Scripture.*

What is your Isaac? May you prove that your faith is genuine by backing it up with action today. Today, you lay Isaac on the altar and trust God with the faith of Abraham, a strong man of God and legendary man of faith.

JOHN 4:43–54

Until I went away to college, my experiences in church had always been pretty predictable. Nothing crazy ever really happened. So, I was fascinated when I met a friend whom we'll call Gertrude. She told us these crazy stories about miraculous and sometimes downright scary things happening in her church's worship services, things that were impossible within the laws of physics. When I would respond with a question even resembling skepticism of her account, or even ask her to back up her claims with Scripture, she would tell me I lacked faith and that my walk with God was just a boring Bible study. Today, she is an avowed and militant atheist. *Read today's Scripture.*

In verses 48–50, Jesus heals this man's son, but criticizes the mind-set of the people in Cana by saying that their faith in God is dependent upon signs and wonders. What happened to "Gertrude's" faith? She ran out of signs and wonders. I have seen God do miraculous things, but my faith is not dependent upon those signs. Resolve today that, even if God doesn't bring about a miracle, your faith in Him will not be shaken. *That* is the faith of a strong man of God.

DAY 60

JOHN 5:1–6

By now, you have seen that Jesus, our ultimate example for masculinity, did not shy away from throwing over tables when He saw injustice in the temple or from speaking the exact words that needed to be spoken to the Samaritan woman in the beginning of chapter 4 and the royal official at the end. He's at it again in *today's Scripture.*

Sometimes, we can become really comfortable in our afflictions and sins. There are worse things, after all, than lying by a pool for thirty-eight years like the man in this story. What are your afflictions or sins? And just as Jesus asked, do you want to be well?

DAY 61

JOHN 5:7–9

Think for a minute on why Jesus asked people such obvious questions as He did in yesterday's text in verse 6. Is it that He genuinely didn't know that the blind person wanted to see, that the lepers wanted to be healed, and that the paralyzed people wanted to walk? I think He asked such questions so that people would answer them. Jesus never healed anyone without that person's permission or someone speaking on his or her behalf. He of course wants to see people healed, but He respects their free will. *Read today's Scripture.*

As many of us do, this man made an excuse in verse 7 and then, just as Jesus does almost every time He heals someone, He told the paralyzed man to *get up*! What a bold thing to say to a paralyzed person! Today, may you get up out of your sin, pick up your excuses, and walk.

PROVERBS 5:21–23

*R*ead today's Scripture. These final three verses of this proverb about the flavorless poison that laces delicious lust and the righteous satisfaction of a husband who is intoxicated with his own wife are a reminder of God's omniscience. To say that God is "omniscient" means that God knows everything. Your ways are in full view of God, and He examines your path.

It is so dangerous for a Christian to become skilled at covering up his tracks, to have no accountability because he has fooled everyone in his life who would hold him accountable. Sometimes, being caught brings a huge sense of relief because we no longer suffer in lonely silence and can finally be real with someone. Someone only truly loves you if he or she knows your flaws and loves you still.

Today, face the realization brought on by these three verses: that you have been caught by God and that He loves you still. Also, confide in your father or male role model about your struggles with lust.

DAY 63

PROVERBS 6:1–11

Mowing grass and doing dishes are the bane of many young men's lives. During the summer, when I was a teenager home from school, my dad would ask me to cut the grass before he left for work. Shortly thereafter, my mom would ask me to do the dishes. Then, quite logically, I would immediately begin playing video games, make plans to go to the beach with my friends, or just go catatonic and lie motionless for hours in front of the TV. *Read today's Scripture.*

Yeah, about that . . . That approach never worked out for me in the end. It would actually end up being *more* work not to do the work right away. As it turns out, grass grows, and the longer you go without cutting it, the bigger a pain it is to deal with—same goes for the dishes. Learn this now and begin implementing it today while the stakes are still low: it is easier to do the work now than it is to do the work later.

DAY 64

PROVERBS 6:12–19

It can be frustrating when you strive to live a godly life. But that frustration is greatly multiplied when you see others—who make no effort whatsoever to honor God or even conduct themselves in a way that is upright—flourish and succeed. Where is God in that seemingly unfair deal? Why doesn't He thwart those who oppose Him and uplift those who serve Him? *Read today's Scripture.*

So, it seems that God is not indifferent on the matter at all. Also, when we read that list, we who serve God have been just like the "villains" at one time or another. You cannot control what non-Christian guys do. You can only control what *you* do, and today you will see to it that you please God by abstaining from (choosing not to participate in) any of these six things that God hates. Read over them one more time (verses 17–19). Don't be frustrated when the wicked prosper. Focus on pleasing God.

DAY 65

JAMES 3:1–12

Read today's Scripture. In no way is hypocrisy more evident than in the mouth of a Christian whose tongue speaks both words of praise to God and profane insults to the people created in God's image (verse 9). Taming the tongue goes beyond just abstaining from cursing. For years and years I struggled with prideful speech (verse 5). When I met someone new, I felt this overwhelming compulsion to make sure he or she knew all the most impressive things about me right away. The funny thing is that this kind of speech actually has the opposite effect, making us look like total goobers. It took God allowing me to fail and be publicly embarrassed by my own bragging for me to finally shut my mouth and learn some humility.

Whether it's through cleaning up your language, becoming more humble, or cutting back on how often you speak, I pray that you learn to tame your tongue the easy way—because learning it the hard way royally stunk!

Day 66

James 3:13–16

Building on yesterday's topic, today we read that wisdom and understanding are demonstrated not so much by the words you say as by the deeds you do. *Read today's Scripture.*

Ouch! My prideful speech was selfish ambition, denying the truth, maybe some bitter envy thrown in there, and here the Bible describes it as "demonic"—meaning I was being demon-like (verse 15)!

Instead, I should have been Christlike. In Jesus' three-year ministry, He actually didn't say all that much that we know of from Scripture. At our student ministry, we taught through all of Jesus' teachings found in all the Gospels, and it took us only one year to finish. When Jesus spoke, it was a big deal, not just because He was God, but because when He spoke He made it really count. No one ever said so much in so few words.

Let your words be few today so that they might increase in value as a result. Replace your words with good deeds done in humility. *That's* evidence of wisdom.

DAY 67

JAMES 3:17–18

As we close this chapter of James, we see that the whole thing ties together with this idea that true wisdom is demonstrated not by words, but by actions. Furthermore, we see the huge influence that the tongue has over the rest of a man. James uses horses, ships, forest fires, animals, poison, springs, figs, and grapes to illustrate this point. I think it's safe to say God *really* wants us to get this concept! *Read today's text.*

Today, let your wisdom be first of all pure, then peace-loving, considerate, submissive, merciful, productive, impartial, and for real. Today, you will make the effort to be a peacemaker. Heads-up: this is going to be tough!

JOHN 5:24–30

The last time we tuned in to our hero Jesus, He had just healed a man who had been paralyzed and lying next to a pool for thirty-eight years. When the Jewish leaders saw this man carrying his mat on the Sabbath, they asked him who told him to do so. The man sold Jesus out, and the plot to kill Jesus gained its initial momentum after Jesus stood up for Himself and stated outright, repetitively, that He is the Son of God and that He and God the Father are One. *Read today's Scripture.*

These teachings are all about crossing over from death to life, and just like John 3:16, they refer to those who believe as having life in the present tense. That means that, though we physically die, as Christians our eternal life really begins the moment we are saved and continues on for eternity!

DAY 69

JOHN 5:31–36

Read today's text. I love how today's text flows perfectly with what we just studied back in James. What Jesus says about Himself in verse 31 is true of you and me as well. When we testify about ourselves and pat our own backs, that's just meaningless bragging in our case. But when we can back it up with action the way Jesus did (verse 36), then those who would tear us down and refuse to believe in us must face the proof of our spotless record.

Today, you're not going to be your own promoter. Instead, you're going to produce undeniable results and let those results, along with the testimony of a John the Baptist or two, speak for you. Also, keep your eyes peeled for an opportunity to be a witness for Jesus just like John the Baptist was. *Boom!*

DAY 70

JOHN 5:37–47

I hope that you have a heart that breaks for the lost. When someone mocks your faith, I hope that the first thing that comes to your mind is the thought that he or she does not know Jesus and is therefore not headed toward heaven right now. I know that's a massively heavy thought. I hope you don't just let it overwhelm or depress you, but I hope it motivates you to speak up on Jesus' behalf the way John the Baptist did. Have you ever wondered what Jesus would say to someone who denies Him as Lord? *Read today's text.*

These words were originally spoken to Jews, and they still apply to Jews today. However, Jesus may have spoken verses 37–38, and 40–44 to someone who has no faith at all. Pray for the lost people in your life, and pray as if you genuinely believe they would spend eternity away from God if they died today.

PROVERBS 6:20–25

Read today's text. Did you catch the word *heart* again in that last verse? Think about what it means to lust in your heart. It's easy to think that lusting after a woman is just something physical, but the heart is involved as well. Your heart is at stake here, and your heart is so precious to your future wife, wherever and whoever she is. Do you remember what I wrote to you about the sexual union being more than a physical act? That's because a man's heart was intended to bond, or "cleave" (Genesis 2:24 KJV), to his wife's heart when their marriage gets its running start on their wedding night.

Repeatedly bonding your heart to someone else's and then ripping it away leaves pieces of your heart with every woman after whom you lust. For the sake of your beautiful future wife, keep your heart from lust. Let your heart be as whole as possible on your wedding night.

DAY 72

PROVERBS 6:26–35

As I toured the country on a bus as a drummer, this guy we'll call Herbert and I were up late one night practicing and talking. Herbert was a little like James Bond in that he got around with women and was therefore somewhat of a walking petri dish (you know, something you put stuff like bacteria and diseases in for scientific experiments). He just sort of dropped this bomb when he said, "I haven't had any feelings for the past twenty or so women I've slept with. I haven't actually cared about a girl in about ten years and probably never will again." What shocked me was that he said this tragic thing as if it were nothing. *Read today's text.*

Unless the Holy Spirit comes into his life, Herbert has lost the ability to bond with women and has developed a reputation like that of the man described in today's text. Don't be like Herbert. In fact, if your name is Herbert, change it.

DAY 73

PROVERBS 8:1–8

Do you have that one friend whose words are usually just, er, made-up? You know that guy who, when he starts to speak, you already know that whatever follows is going to be about as beneficial to hear as the mating call of an ostrich that has bronchitis? If you're having a hard time thinking of someone . . . then there's a chance that you're that guy. Anyway, *read today's Scripture.*

Today, open your lips to speak what is true, what is right. Speak justly with impartial fairness toward everyone. Be a man whose words are trustworthy and honorable. This may require you to pretend that there is something extremely interesting about the ceiling when the raunchy jokes start in the locker room today.

DAY 74

JAMES 4:1-3

This passage is the answer to a question that gnaws and claws at the hearts of *several* Christians. If you commit it to memory today, you will not only *not* be one of those Christians, but you will be the Christian who can finally bring some relieving wisdom to the others. *Read today's text.*

If that were not in the Bible, you could sell it and become a billionaire. There it is: the reason straight out of God's Word as to why some people do not receive that for which they so adamantly pray or that for which they so anxiously long, but never articulate to God. To receive something from God, you have to ask God for it, and you have to ask Him for it with motives that align with His, not the selfish aspects of your own.

DAY 75

JAMES 4:4–5

To appreciate today's passage, you need to understand the nature of God's righteous jealousy. It is not the petty envy of a childish god, but the justified indignation of the God who gave His life for those who are forsaking Him. *Read today's text.*

God has the right to force us to pick sides this way because of what He has done and because of who He is. This passage, by the way, is not a command to make enemies of the world. Rather, it is a command not to forsake God in favor of the world. As a Christian, your sins have been atoned for by the sacrifice of Jesus, and you have been filled with the Holy Spirit of God. Heads-up: this may mean that you will find yourself rejected by the world from time to time, but it is far better to be rejected by the world than condemned for your sins in judgment before God.

DAY 76

JAMES 4:6

Our last devotional should have been pretty humbling, but in case it wasn't, here's *today's Scripture.*

Wow! Think about that. If you are proud, then the God who created the entire universe—including its volcanoes, great white sharks, and mountains—with the words that came from His all-powerful mouth is *opposed to you.* Um, yeah . . . things don't look so good for you if you are a proud guy.

I don't know about you, but I for one am incredibly grateful for the grace that God gives us as described in this verse. Do you want God's favor today? Then, according to God, you should humble yourself, if you haven't already. Come to fully realize as much as you can who God is and who you are. If you have any self-awareness at all and any concept of who God is at all, the only logical response is humility.

DAY 77

JOHN 6:1–9

Because of His many miracles, Jesus had a massive crowd following Him. However, people who follow Jesus for His miracles may not actually believe in Him for who He claims to be, but just for the sake of the miracles themselves. Which are you? Even among his disciples were those who watched and those who believed. Again, which are you? *Read today's text.*

There they are again: Philip and Andrew. This time, they're telling Jesus why He can't possibly do what He intends to do and asking Him questions about how He intends to do it. Once again, in verse 5, Jesus asks a question to which He already knows the answer, thereby giving Philip the chance to show great faith. Philip fails. I can almost hear the feigned desperation in Jesus' voice.

What does the hungry crowd best represent in your life? Has it yet occurred to you that, just like Jesus in verse 6, God already knows what He's going to do about it?

DAY 78

JOHN 6:10–11

Read today's text. Did the grass mentioned in verse 10 grow there because the crowd following Jesus was approaching, or did God cause it to grow there in preparation for the crowd? I don't know and neither will you, this side of heaven. Did you notice that verse 10 only counts the men? As we learned in chapter 4, this was an era in which women were not respected as they should have been. So, this crowd could easily have been over 15,000!

In verse 11, after they were seated, the Son gave thanks to the Father. He then not only gave them as much bread as they wanted, but thereafter did the same with the fish. God takes limited resources, like our experience, intelligence, and finances, and achieves with them something far beyond the sum of their parts. Ask God to accomplish something in you today that is beyond the total of your ability so that you may know that He accomplished it.

JOHN 6:12–13

God's Word is filled with number trends, including the numbers twelve and seven most prominently. Twelve is the number of tribes in the nation of Israel, and seven is considered the perfect number. In the book of Revelation, both numbers come up all the time in the passages describing the architecture of heaven. *Read today's Scripture.*

Boom! There were twelve baskets left over, and there is no way you'll convince me that was accidental or coincidental. After all, one person could have eaten the whole original meal, so I know that the remainder divided into twelve was intentional on God's part. Also, Jesus waited until everyone had enough to eat. How do you fill twelve baskets with five loaves? You supernaturally multiply what you started with. Jesus still does this today with our own gifts and abilities: *He takes the loaves and fishes that we have and does something greater with them.* What does the fact that Jesus not only waited until people were satisfied, but also multiplied the original amount reveal about the nature of God?

Day 80

Proverbs 8:9–11

Today, we raise the stakes on our quest for wisdom as strong men of God. Honestly, just how important is wisdom to you right now? According to the wisest *and richest* man who ever lived, wisdom is worth more than riches. *Read today's text.*

To fully appreciate the weight of this verse, you have to understand just how historically rich Solomon was. Earning 666 talents of gold per year (one talent is 34.5 kilograms which converts to 1,109 troy ounces) and assuming the value of gold to be $1,000 per ounce, he earned about $740 million per year over forty years, which comes to about $30 billion by the end of his career! This man who lived several millennia ago would still make a world's richest list if he were alive today. And he said that "*nothing desirable*" can compare with wisdom! So, if you find yourself distracted by worldly possessions at the moment, take it from one of the richest men in history: you would rather have wisdom.

DAY 81

PROVERBS 8:12–14

Let's have a quick vocabulary lesson before today's Scripture reading. *Prudence* (NIV) is the conviction to rule one's self according to reason and logic. *Discretion* is the authority to rule over one's own private money and affairs. *Read today's text.*

To have insight is to have power, and these words were written by the most insightful and powerful man of his day. Sound judgment is probably not the most prominent thing among your peers—who apparently like to film their bathroom endeavors and post the resulting footage to YouTube—but the fact that you are pursuing wisdom and therefore sound judgment gives you strength according to verse 14. Aspire today to be the wisest among your peers, keeping in mind as you do that wisdom and arrogance or condescension are not at all the same thing. Remember also what we've learned from the book of James on the value of being men of few words.

DAY 82

PROVERBS 8:15–21

Read today's Scripture. Chances are that being a king or prince is not exactly in the cards for you, but being a godly man of influence most definitely is. How do godly men of influence get their wisdom? They get it from God's Word and make their decisions accordingly. Verse 18 describes how wisdom brings about wealth, while verse 19 describes how much more valuable wisdom is than wealth. So, if you strive for godly wisdom and attain it, you will also gain wealth along the way. But you'll be happier that you've attained wisdom! Did you also notice verse 18's mention of "lasting wealth"? Too often, when people without wisdom find themselves wealthy, they then lose everything in a few short months. So, may you (as verses 17–18 so alluringly say) seek wisdom that you may find not only wisdom, but everything that comes with it!

DAY 83

JAMES 4:7

My dad is massive. He stands an intimidating six feet four inches tall, and as a little dude growing up, I was convinced that nothing in this world, aside from God, could take on my dad—with the exception perhaps of the prehistoric shark known as the megalodon (more specifically, a megalodon on a good day). So, it was pretty natural growing up to submit to his authority, but his strength also brought with it a sense of security from those who would do my family harm. *Read today's text.*

The power of God is incomprehensible. If you have a smartphone or tablet, download the Google Sky Map and explore the universe for a second right now. Let me know when you're done. Ready? Okay, *God spoke all of that and incomprehensibly more into existence.* This awesome power is beyond Satan and is intimidating to Satan. So, let's submit to God and, filled with God's Holy Spirit, know that the devil will flee when we resist him.

DAY 84

JAMES 4:8

We are about to get all theological in this devotional book, yo. *Read today's Scripture.*

As a follower of Christ, you have the capacity to come near to God as this verse says. Furthermore, when you do come near to God—be that through worship, prayer, or getting into His Word—*God comes near to you.* That is the most epic thing you will learn today, even if you watch one of those 1980s National Geographic videos where everyone wears acid-washed jeans that stop just short of their white tennis shoes. Who are we that God would draw near to us?

If you know who you are and know who God is, then the only reasonable thing to do is wash your hands and purify your heart because we are sinners drawing near to the holy and perfect God, who judges the universe! Now would be a great time to do exactly what verse 8 says to do.

DAY 85

JAMES 4:9–10

Read today's Scripture. Being broken before God is the opposite of being prideful or even having your act at all together before God. It is an ancient (and I mean back to the days when the psalms were written), traditional state of worship before God. When the prophet Isaiah (my son Aiden's middle name) saw God in a vision in Isaiah 6, his first response was one of woe and self-loathing. He responded this way because he was aware of his sin and, as a result of this vision, way more aware of God's greatness.

Brokenness is a logical response when we encounter our holy God. Contrary to what some male stereotypes would have you believe, weeping before God in worship is one of the manliest things you could do; the man who weeps before God is the man who knows who he is and has a clue who God is. The next time you worship God, be humbly broken before Him, and He will lift you up.

DAY 86

JOHN 6:14–15

Because of the rampant misinterpretations of the messianic (having to do with the Messiah) prophecies throughout the Old Testament, many prominent Jews in Jesus' day were expecting the Messiah to be some military general who would show up on the scene with an intense bloodlust and liberate Israel from the rule of the Roman Empire. Instead, Jesus showed up not only having been raised in the Podunk town of Nazareth, but also having been born out of what community consensus seemed to confirm was a teenage pregnancy out of wedlock. These elements don't exactly make up the backstory to a prophesied king. Not only that, Jesus had this habit of disappearing on people. *Read today's text.*

If Jesus had the habit of withdrawing to quiet places to be by Himself and get alone with God, then you and I absolutely ought to keep the same habit. Stick with it!

DAY 87

JOHN 6:16–21

In your life, the strong winds blow, and the waters grow rough. *Read today's Scripture.*

The disciples left the craziness of the mass feeding without Jesus. In fact, they actually rowed three or four miles without Him. Have you ever left without Jesus? What happened when you left Him? Are you in such a state now? If so, I'll bet it's dark, just as it was for the disciples in verse 17. I'll bet that you are overwhelmed, just as the disciples were by the strong winds and rough waters.

My student, the strong winds and rough waters will come. Being a disciple of Jesus is no guarantee that difficulty will not visit you. In fact, whether or not you'll have difficulty is not the question. Rather, the question is, will your faith in Him remain intact in the midst of the storm?

The storm surrounds you, but Jesus approaches. Do you see Him? Be willing to take Him into the boat. You might see—as the disciples did in one of the more understated of Jesus' miracles (verse 21)—that you are suddenly safely where you want to be, simply in the presence of Jesus. He is with you in the midst of the storm.

DAY 88

JOHN 6:22–24

*R*ead today's Scripture. I kind of like this crowd's style. Granted, we will learn on Day 95 that their motivation came more from their stomachs than their faith, but I still love the way they hunted Jesus down. Do likewise today, young man. With the eyes of a hunter stalking its prey, scan the horizon to see precisely where God is at work, and let no body of water or obstacle, no matter how vast or discouraging, stop you from getting to HIm.

Though being in the center of God's will and at the epicenter of where God is working isn't always the safest place to be, it is the best place to be. Is God moving in your church's homeless ministry? Guess what: you just became that ministry's most avid volunteer. Are people being saved through your church's Upward ministry? Guess what: you just enlisted as a referee. Row as far as you must to meet Jesus where He is working, even if that means putting yourself in harm's way.

DAY 89

PROVERBS 8:22–36

Today's passage is like a personal soliloquy spoken by wisdom directly to your face. *Read today's text.*

Are any of your problems more immovable than the mountains and hills of the earth (verse 25), deeper than the ocean (verse 27), or taller than the height at which the clouds hover above the earth (verse 28)? I didn't think so. Get this: according to this proverb, God established for you the wisdom necessary to overcome your trials before He created those imposing mountains, that unfathomable ocean, or those seemingly unreachable clouds.

Seek wisdom, strong young man of God, and find both life and favor from the Lord today (verse 35). Seek wisdom from your Bible and the advisors God has placed in your life. Let not your heart be daunted by these trials. Instead, let your trials be daunted by your God, who is the Maker of the mountains, oceans, and skies.

DAY 90

PROVERBS 7:1–10

Today, you will steer clear of anything that might entice you to lust. In today's text, Solomon slams the young man who goes near her house, knowing exactly where he's going, and doing so at a time when he is not likely to be discovered. Verse 7 says that this young man has no sense. Ha! *Read today's Scripture.*

What happens when you go where pornography and lust may be found? They come out to meet you, armed with all of their craftiness and experience in luring in young men like you (verse 10). Go figure. Why don't we stay away from the adulteress's house (smartphones, tablets, computers, magazines, whatever) today. You are, after all, a strong young man of God who, unlike this guy in today's text, actually has sense enough to know what happens when you knock on temptation's door. Ready, set, *fast from technology*!

DAY 91

PROVERBS 7:10–23

The hidden truth about pornography is what it will cost you. This is consistent with the nature of all of Satan's traps. *Read today's text, and please read verses 22 and 23 a few times over again.*

The idea of pornography costing you your life seems overly dramatic—and that is precisely Satan's intention, to downplay and cover up just how cancerous pornography is. It rewires your brain to sabotage it so that it can never be satisfied sexually. Such reprogramming is *bad news* for the young man of God who has the finish line of marriage on his mind. Such distortion of God's perfect design will cost you more in the long run than you can possibly imagine right now.

I know that this is heavy, but it needs to be shared. I have counseled many people, including married men, who have independently from one another shared with me that, on nights when they look at pornography, their children and spouses have night terrors. Wake up and smell the Proverbs. Satan is all over this, and this sin will cost you your life.

DAY 92

JAMES 4:11–12

Today's text uses the phrase "brothers and sisters" (*adelphos* in Greek) to refer to your fellow Christians. Also, I would like the world to know that I just did the dishes for the fifth time this week. That has nothing to do with this particular devotional, but I wanted to share it. Now, *read today's text*.

When you slam your fellow Christian, whose sins have been atoned for by the blood of Jesus, you presume yourself to be the judge, but as it turns out, that seat has been taken by God. Verse 12 checks our pride by reminding us that we sinners before the Lawgiver and Judge have no business giving out laws and judging, especially when we would be found guilty of breaking those laws and offending that Judge. Instead of passing judgment or speaking with condescension to our fellow Christians today, let's strive deliberately to lift them up.

DAY 93

JAMES 4:13–16

*R*ead today's text. At this phase of life, people begin to shape their visions for the future, and that is a great thing. However, it is imperative that you lay all of your plans before the throne of your King and say, "God, if it is Your will, this plan is the desire of my heart." Otherwise, *and please do not forget this*, God will thwart and righteously sabotage the plans that we lay in interference with His plans for our lives. Oh, how countless are the frustrated men of God who assume lordship over their own lives after having confessed Jesus as Lord (Romans 10:9).

If Jesus is Lord in your life, that means that you are not. Instead of insisting on your will, prefer God's. Test and approve any opportunity that might be God's will, but do so in a state of worship (Romans 12:1–2). It's hard to mess up that way.

DAY 94

JAMES 4:17

Buck up and get ready, because on a scale from one to über-convicting, today's singular verse is über-convicting. *Read today's Scripture.*

Boom. According to this verse, it can be a sin *not* to do something. Funny, huh? We usually think of sin in terms of "thou shalt not," but it is just as often "thou should have." According to Ephesians 2:10, God has laid out good works for you to do, and if you knowingly miss those opportunities, you sin. Be steadfast in your preemptive (that means before stuff happens) decision right here and now as you sit on your beanbag/hand-me-down chair/screaming little brother that you will not commit the sin of letting that opportunity to do good pass you by. Also, please get off of your little brother.

DAY 95

JOHN 6:25–27

Do you remember the crowd of people who rowed all the way to Capernaum to track down Jesus? Jesus is about to address them in *today's text*.

Are you working for food that spoils? Will the fulfillment of the biggest goal you have right now (by the way, it's an issue if you have none) last longer than eternity? If not, then you might have been a part of this hungry crowd that followed Jesus not because they believed He was Lord, but because He was like a talking bread dispenser to them. So, are you chasing after Jesus for what He can give you or because you believe that He is the risen Son of God and Lord of your life?

List your goals right now and let those whose fulfillment will last for eternity (such as leading your Andrew and Phillip to Christ) be at the top of the list.

DAY 96

JOHN 6:28–29

In our previous devotional, Jesus showed the crowd He had just fed that their reasons for following Him were the wrong reasons. This crowd was obsessed with bread that would eventually spoil, and Jesus told them to focus on eternal things that would never spoil. *Read today's text.*

It may have been that this crowd was of a Jewish background and therefore tied to the idea that pleasing God meant completing a series of works, or it may have been that they just wanted more bread. Either way, Jesus lays out something shocking: the only work we need to complete in order to see God do something eternal in our lives is not a work at all but a belief.

Most people outside of the church and countless people within it still believe as this crowd did. Today, you will clear that up. As Paul writes exhaustively in Romans 10, the work of salvation has already been completed by Jesus. We need only to believe. Spread the word!

DAY 97

JOHN 6:30–35

The manna that fell down from heaven was more than just God's provision for another day in the Israelites' exodus. It was prophetic (meaning it foretold) of the way God would provide one day by sending Jesus down from heaven. *Read today's Scripture.*

This crowd loves bread as much as my wife does, and that is more than Jesus (just kidding, kind of). Also, they are demanding signs of Jesus before they would put their faith in Him, and as I laid out on Day 59, a faith that is dependent on signs and wonders is a weak faith. It is as though they are trying to make a deal with Jesus by offering Him their faith in exchange for . . . wait for it . . . *more stinking bread*. Jesus' response, however, is a beautiful statement guaranteeing the permanence of the believer's salvation.

DAY 98

PROVERBS 7:24–27

Take a minute to pray for your Pharisees. Have you lived out a Christian life with integrity and demonstrated God's love for them? These are two undeniable apologetics (proofs) of God. *Read today's passage*.

The number of young men who are caught up in and being poisoned by pornography and the adulterous compromising of their purity before marriage is incalculable. Realize in this moment that such spiritual carnage breaks God's heart. Similarly, let your heart be filled with compassion for your brothers who are being spiritually annihilated by the sin of lust. I personally know a guy who used to call himself a Christian until he just got tired of being defeated by this temptation and left the church altogether. Today, he is a practicing Satanist.

Pray now for all the saints, just as Ephesians 1:14–16 and 6:18 tell us to, and consider that you might be called to the ministry of helping your brothers out of this mess that is lust.

DAY 99

PROVERBS 9:1–6

God makes men free. In fact, the first three words that God spoke to mankind were, "You are free" Genesis 2:16. Man is free. He is free to sin, free to be dumb, and—if he gas given his life to Jesus—free to love God. All the while, God's wisdom cries out to man. *Read today's Scripture.*

We cannot say, when everything has fallen apart, that God did not give us guidance. It is not as though God is keeping His wisdom a secret. For crying out loud, the Bible is the best-selling book of all time and has been published almost throughout the entire world. Now, that means that you and I are responsible to act upon the wisdom that God has made so invitingly available to us. Because wisdom is so plainly made known to us, because wisdom sets a table and invites us, and because together in this book we have feasted on it, we are obligated to live in accordance with it. Excuses will not fly with God now that you are being made wise by His Word, so make none today.

DAY 100

PROVERBS 9:7–9

Strong young men of God speak with candor (meaning they say what needs to be said even if it isn't a pleasant thing to say), but they also have the wisdom to know when not to speak. There are some people who will not listen to you as you share God's wisdom, and that is on *them*. Refrain from the futile quest to alter the behavior of someone who is mocking you, especially if that person is ungodly. *Read today's text.*

When it comes to stepping into discussions with those described as "mockers" in verse 7, I only do so if I can present the gospel or correct a misrepresentation of what the Bible says. That is at the core of this passage: are you teachable? Can you take correction and do so with gratitude? The ability to take instruction well is a sign of wisdom.

DAY 101

JAMES 5:1–6

Come to the point at which you can truthfully say to God, "If You blessed me with great wealth, I would give generously." Say that aloud, and say it until you know that God knows that you genuinely mean it. Don't *read today's text* until you do.

This chapter points out how silly it is to be greedy in light of the fact that Jesus will come back one day. The oppressors in these verses were common in the first century and Old Testament days. They lured in workers to pull off massive projects with the promise of great pay, but then denied the workers payment when the project was complete. They wanted wealth at the cost of their souls.

If you are not generous with what money you have now, you will not be generous if God blesses you with great wealth. Prove yourself trustworthy with little, so that you may be entrusted with much if it's God's will. Then, you will not suffer verses 1–3.

P.S. You could totally use verse 4 if people fail to pay you for mowing their grass!

DAY 102

JAMES 5:7–8

It is by design that we do not know when Jesus is coming back. The timing is such a massive secret that, according to Matthew 24:36, even Jesus didn't know! This way, we have to evangelize as though Jesus could come back any second. Also, it helps us make sense of the bad things that happen in our lives. We can—because Jesus will come soon to make everything right—wait patiently on His return trusting that we will one day live in perfection. *Read today's text.*

Stand firm, young man. Though evil triumphs at times, its day of destruction is coming in Revelation 20:10. Trust that God will bring our enemy the devil to justice for what he has done.

DAY 103

JAMES 5:9

Though strong young men of God are willing to stand alone for the gospel, they need brothers in Christ. They need fellowship in a church. Here's the thing about churches, though: they are full of imperfect people. There are two ways for a church to function. One, a church could be filled exclusively with people who are without flaw and without sin. Two, a church could be filled with people who forgive one another. If you have never been let down by the church before, just give it time. *Read today's text.*

God our Judge is standing at the door. He hears what we say about His beloved children when we grumble against one another. Furthermore, our brothers and sisters in Christ will soon have something to grumble about us if they don't already. Be faithful to your church, despite the flawed people there, just as they should be faithful to you despite your flaws.

DAY 104

JOHN 6:36–38

You need to be at least somewhat knowledgeable of a discussion that has been going on among Christians for two millennia: exactly how is it that people are saved? On one side of the discussion, Calvinists believe that God chooses who is saved and therefore who is not. On the other side of the discussion, Arminians believe that a man alone decides whether or not he is saved. Many people plant their flags tentatively somewhere in between these two schools of thought.

Wherever you plant yours, you need to know two things that are shown to us in *today's text.*

First, God draws people to be saved. Second, those who come to God will never be driven away. Whether you are a Calvinist, Arminian, Molinist, Remonstrant, or just a drummer like me, you have to see the beautiful compassion of our God, in whom we can find security for our salvation if we believe.

DAY 105

JOHN 6:39-40

I've always been fascinated with the Bible's theme of resurrection from the dead, but as the father of a son who passed away, I now have a more passionate desire than ever to see these teachings realized in my life. This teaching has to do with all believers throughout the course of human history being raised to life together. It is about a beautiful reunion, my reunion with my son Aiden. With whom do you long to be reunited?

Most directly, this text is a clear-cut statement of God's will for you and everyone you know. *Read today's text.*

Memorize verse 40 and use this as an answer to the question "How could a loving God send people to hell?" It's not God's will that anyone go to hell but that all men come to believe in Him and be saved (2 Peter 3:9 and 1 Timothy 2:3-4)!

DAY 106

JOHN 6:41-42

When I started out in ministry, my first job was at the church in which I was raised. From what I understand (based on conflicting reports), as a little dude I would sprint through the fellowship hall during Wednesday night meals, screaming at the top of my lungs, and do other things that might cause people to not take me seriously as an adult. It took a while for the people who had changed my diapers to actually believe I had something worthwhile for them to hear. *Please, read today's text.*

A shift may be taking place in the way you perceive yourself. It is a good thing that you start to see yourself as a man, but it can be difficult when adults who have known you your whole life don't see you the way you feel you ought to be seen. Listen: Jesus dealt with this too, so don't sweat it too much. Respect will come from undeniable results, time, or just relocating.

DAY 107

PROVERBS 9:10–12

Read today's Scripture. To have "fear of the LORD" is to have a proper respect for the Almighty Creator, and according to this passage, it is also to have the beginning of wisdom. A proper fear and respect for God is an excellent basis for wisdom because it is wisdom built upon the only complete theory for just how the universe came into existence, the only complete sense of morality (knowing right from wrong) in our world, and the only authoritative and historically consistent ancient historical document: our Bible.

Consider the sages, the old-timers of the Christian faith. Take a close look at the lives of the gray-haired men in your church who have been walking with Christ for decades longer than you have been alive. See how God has rewarded them, see the proof of this proverb lived out for you, and aspire to have the same testimony when your hair turns gray.

DAY 108

PROVERBS 9:13–18

Like Grandpa Adam and Granny Eve, we tend to be drawn to things just because they are forbidden. I once counseled a teenage girl with her parents. The parents had posted a list of ten rules on the refrigerator. By the time this family had arrived at my office, this girl had broken number nine. She was working her way down the list in order. *Read today's text.*

This classic error of humanity that draws us to drink waters simply because they are stolen and eat food in secret simply for the secrecy of it is evidence of an old doctrine known as the "total depravity of man." Just as Romans 3:23 says, "All have sinned and fall short of the glory of God."

Today, silently study your classmates. I'd wager that it will not take long for you to hear the students of folly. They tend to be loud, after all. Most important, humbly take note of the ways in which you are similar.

DAY 109

PROVERBS 10:1–5

If you were to write today's Scripture for an assignment in school, your teacher might tell you that you lack focus, but he or she would be wrong. Though they may seem disjunctive, these verses circle around the common theme of work ethic. *Read today's Scripture.*

Verses 2, 3, and 5 speak to the satisfaction that comes from accomplishing something through your own hard work. This is why verse 2 says that righteousness in this context delivers you from death: you have the ability to stay alive. Think hard about verse 3 and analyze your own memories. God denies the cravings of the wicked. Have any of your cravings been denied in the past? Think also about verse 5. Is this a time of harvest for you, and if so, are you letting opportunity die?

DAY 110

JAMES 5:10–11

The man with weak faith might think that a compassionate and merciful God would spare those who love him any difficulty or trial whatsoever. That man would be wrong and completely ignorant of the Bible. Not you, my student! *Read today's text.*

Let the same be said of you as you show great patience in the midst of suffering. It is a blessing to have persevered, and the act of persevering in itself will inspire faith in others. As my wife and I prayed each day that our son Aiden would live, one thing that helped was the steady flow of reports that other Christians and even non-Christians were learning vicariously through our experiences. As you show patience in your suffering, let this be your objective: to demonstrate how a Christian man responds to trial.

DAY 111

JAMES 5:12

Read today's Scripture. Our culture refers to "swearing" in the same sense as using profanity, but this verse is different. Here, "swear" is referring to the taking of an oath while evoking the honor or value of something or someone. For example, "I swear on Elmo's goldfish that I did not eat your pogo stick."

This is a call to let your word alone be as strong as a promise. Prove that when you say the word *yes*, and say it only once, you mean it. As the last phrase of this verse shows, once you let the integrity of your word be compromised, people may have reason to question everything else you say and thereby condemn you. Think for a minute on how effective a James 5:12 man is in evangelism. Think also on how frequently or infrequently such a man speaks.

DAY 112

JAMES 5:13–16

At the end of this devotional, you will pray for your Andrew, Philip, and Pharisees, but first you will read one of the most amazing verses in the Bible about prayer. *Read today's Scripture.*

If you are not familiar with this ecclesial (having to do with the church) tradition, the elders are the older sage men of faith who lead and protect the church. When a band of righteous men pray in great faith, God does great things. Sometimes, your prayers are not answered because they are simply not in accordance with the will of God, but other times it is because you lack the faith of an elder. Sometimes, you are sick because you like to lick door handles, but other times it is because of sin. In any case, wouldn't you like your prayers to be powerful and effective? Then strive to be a righteous man.

Confess your sins to a fellow Christian man, align your heart with God, and then pray a powerful and effective prayer for the Andrew, Philip, and Pharisees in your life.

DAY 113

JOHN 6:43–47

Speaking of faith, it takes faith to believe in the Father whom we have not seen. *Read today's Scripture.*

Again, we see that God the Father draws people to be saved (verse 44) and we also see the necessity of belief to be saved (verse 47). The theological idea running through these verses is an extremely important one, and that is: God is sovereign. The word *sovereign* can be broken in two to mean that God "so reigns," meaning He reigns in this way or that way. The sovereignty of God is important because it means that God is in charge and sits on the throne with the authority and ability to change things to be His way. If God were not sovereign, then none of His love or power would mean a thing because He would be unable to use either.

As a Christian, take a moment to thank God the Father for the gift He gave when He drew you to be saved (Ephesians 2:8).

DAY 114

JOHN 6:48–59

Today, we read what I affectionately like to call Jesus' "Zombie Discourse." It's about to get weird, fellas. *Read today's text.*

Jesus often spoke in parables and deeply enigmatic messages like this. They always went right over the Pharisees' heads because they took His metaphorical words literally (verse 52). They actually thought Jesus was saying, "Eat Me." Rather, Jesus was prophesying about communion, an act of remembrance the church does together because it believes that Jesus' body was broken on the cross (the bread we eat) and His blood was spilled on our behalf (the wine or grape juice we drink).

The first time Jesus said it, the Zombie Discourse took serious faith on the part of the disciples, but everything came into focus after the resurrection when they realized the Zombie Discourse was Jesus' faith-testing way of describing communion before there really was communion . . . or the "Lord's Supper."

DAY 115

JOHN 6:60–66

Some of the bread lovers from way back at the feeding of the five thousand are *still* lingering in the crowd that follows Jesus. While many ministry leaders do absolutely whatever they can to keep from scaring people away, Jesus' teachings here are partially intended to get rid of the fakers in the crowd. *Read today's Scripture.*

Of those present at the Zombie Discourse, the false disciples who took Jesus' spiritual words to be literal said in verse 60, "This teaching is hard! Who can accept it?" No kidding. That's a hard teaching if you think Jesus is speaking in physical terms! Good grief! Did they think Jesus would ask them to put bibs on next and take a bite of Him wherever they would like? I *love* Jesus' response in verse 61. As ridiculous as that interpretation is, I have personally encountered atheists who actually quoted this passage to me thinking exactly as the false disciples did.

These false disciples turned back in verse 66 as soon as they had a hard time understanding Jesus, and none of them had fooled Jesus for a second. Keep your eyes peeled over your own youth group: verse 66 happens every day.

DAY 116

PROVERBS 10:6-7

These two verses do the whole split thing that many proverbs do with two lines each describing the opposite of one another, but there are two common denominators between them. Both associate the righteous with blessings. *Check it out.*

Righteousness is more than following a list of rules. Righteousness flows from a heart that longs to obey God. Righteousness is not always popular. It might make you stand out, and it might make other people uncomfortable, but it brings awesome blessings. The strong young man of God leads an uncompromising life of righteousness.

BE UNCOMPROMISING.

DAY 117

PROVERBS 10:8-9

Verse 8 reiterates two things we have already discussed, but it is of course worth rereading. Verse 9, however, reminds me of a great story. *Read today's Scripture.*

I was drumming in this group, and it came to light that some of the members may have been smoking pot and would be cut from the group. People around the room seemed to squirm when the staff sat us down to investigate, but I pulled out my phone and started playing a game. They all knew I took my Christian faith seriously, and the director of the group actually pointed out the fact that I was so secure (verse 9) that I had nothing to worry about but winning the game on my phone. He was right. Covering your tracks is exhausting. Walking in integrity is awesome and gets you ridiculously high scores on your phone games.

DAY 118

PROVERBS 10:10-14

A collection of proverbs on the effects of our words is *always* helpful for this phase of life.

Read today's text. I love verse 11's imagery of a righteous person's mouth as a fountain overflowing with words of life itself. People want to go to such a fountain. They draw near to it. Let your words be exactly that. I pray that people are drawn to you so that they can hear your words because you have stored up knowledge (verse 14) to be shared. Furthermore, if you are also a loving person, then that love will cover a multitude of wrongs (verse 12 and 1 Peter 4:8).

Let your imagination paint in your mind right now a vision of others approaching you with expectant faces. They want to hear words of life from you, and they know that you are a loving person. See it now, and take corrective steps today to make that vision a reality.

Day 119

James 5:17–18

The last time we were in James, we saw that the prayer of a righteous man is powerful and effective. Today, we see an Old Testament example in Elijah; the implications for this example are utterly immense. *Read today's Scripture.*

Elijah (my oldest son's middle name) was a prophet who saw some of the most amazing miracles of the entire Bible. He stood alone against more than four hundred prophets of the false god Baal at Mount Carmel and won decisively in a showdown to determine whose faith was legit. When this guy prayed, God changed weather patterns—*weather patterns*—for him. The meteorological conditions and the course of human history were drastically altered at the behest of a man's prayer.

May you be such a man of faith, and may you spend at least the next ten minutes trying to wrap your head around the theological implications (including how God exists within or outside of time) of the fact that God changed the course of history because a man asked him to. I'll give you a hint: one of them is that prayer changes things.

DAY 120

JAMES 5:19–20

Did the verse I warned you about come true? The one in which people who were false disciples walked away (you know: John 6:66)? (Creepy reference number, huh?) If so, brace up because you're about to go after them. *Read today's verses.*

There is only so much you can do, but that is exactly how much you will do: as much as you can. You will attempt to be a prodigal retriever today. You will approach the one who has drifted away from the church and drifted away from the truth. If you can pull this off, you will save that person from spiritual (and possibly physical) death and cover a multitude of sins. So, any social awkwardness that might result is a small price to pay for such a worthy endeavor. Go now and James 5:20 someone. (Yes, I just turned a Scripture reference into a verb.)

Day 121

1 Peter 1:1–2
(Woo-hoo! A new book begins!)

The book you are about to start was once highly illegal; you would have been killed violently for having a copy of it. It was written to the underground church that was being persecuted by Rome's crazy, evil, and decidedly Christian-hating emperor named Nero. This letter had to be smuggled in to Rome, and the believers who first read it were outlaws. *Read today's Scripture.*

Again, we see the sovereignty of God (see Day 113) in verses 1 and 2. These regions in verse 1 are all over modern-day Turkey, which is once again persecuting Christians today, and by "today" I literally mean the exact day I'm writing this.

When Christians were caught, sometimes Nero would have them mounted upside down to massive wooden stakes in his garden, cover them in wax except for their faces, and light their feet on fire to light his garden. So, that's nice. It was these people to whom Peter wrote, "May grace and peace be multiplied to you." Wow.

DAY 122

1 PETER 1:3-4

As you will see, these verses are the first of many in this book in which Peter points these beleaguered Christians' minds toward heaven to keep them motivated. What else do you say to people who are losing everything and watching things get even worse? *Read today's Scripture.*

We used to have this little sports car. It was wicked quick, and it had a robotic extending and retracting rear wing, which I never ceased to think was insanely cool. This thing was a blast. It was also a massive pain in the pancreas. It broke down constantly, took ridiculously expensive oil that was about a hundred dollars a bottle, required parts to be shipped from a Mercedes plant in Germany, and rode on tires that could only be bought from a mythological tire shop that emerged from the ground every other equinox. That car was definitely a treasure that perished, spoiled, and faded.

The living hope of Jesus' resurrection and the fruits of an evangelistic life are eternal treasures kept in heaven that never fade and therefore are far more worthy pursuits than the treasures of this life—even if said treasures have robotic extending wings (Matthew 6:20).

DAY 123

1 PETER 1:5

The original recipients of 1 Peter met in various hidden congregations all over Rome. Some would meet on the outskirts of town, while some met in catacombs, which are open graves beneath the streets. If they were caught, they would be arrested and likely executed with no chance at a fair trial. Their emperor, after all, was crazy. He burned huge portions of Rome and blamed it on Christians to spread an inspired hatred of them, and it worked for a while. *Read today's text.*

Though they lived in a constant state of imminent danger, they were shielded through faith. In Ephesians 6:16, we see that faith is the shield with which we extinguish the fiery darts of the evil one. Can you relate to these Christians in 1 Peter? Are you being assailed by Satan's arrows? Then take up the shield of faith and *stubbornly* persevere. Resolve now that you will not back down from your love of God.

DAY 124

JOHN 6:67–71

Meanwhile, back with Jesus and His dwindling number of disciples (and by "meanwhile," I mean about thirty years earlier), Jesus had just dropped this teaching bomb that caused the false disciples to scatter. He turns to the twelve and asks them a question. *Read today's Scripture.*

I love Peter's response in verses 68 and 69 because they prove that Peter was truly saved. Even in the face of confusing teaching, Peter knew that Jesus' words were those of life and He was the Holy One of God. In fact, he uses the words, "We have come to *believe* and *know*" (emphasis mine).

Are you at one of those points right now where it is really hard to tell what God is doing, and people seem to be leaving? Did your youth pastor just go to another church or join a traveling group of yodeling contortionists (a common problem in the Midwest)? I pray that you would respond to this confusing time the way that Peter did.

DAY 125

JOHN 7:1–5

Watch this bubbling plot to kill Jesus get hotter at the Festival of Shelters. This was a massive bring-your-own-tent party that lasted several days, and as siblings do when the family is trying to get out the door to go somewhere, Jesus' brothers taunt Him. *Read today's Scripture.*

If you'd recall, our own James, whose book we recently finished, was one of these brothers doing the taunting! Perhaps they genuinely did want to see Jesus prove Himself to them, or perhaps they were just mocking Him. Either way, the text says they didn't believe in Him.

If your family does not believe in you, my heart goes out to you. I don't know how you deal with it! Let it be a comfort to you, though, that you have something in common with Jesus, and may you not only come to learn how you might deal with your family by doing as Jesus does here, but may you also come to know Jesus a little more personally because of what you have in common.

DAY 126

JOHN 7:6–11

Our imaginations can only conjure a vague semblance of what it was like inside Jesus' head when He faced threats of death on the earth. What we can see, based on His actions, is a constant awareness of the Father's ultimate plan and a desire to see that plan come to fruition, no matter what others thought of Him. I think that is another aspect of Jesus worth imitating. *Read today's text.*

According to verse 7, the world can't hate you if you never testify about its works as evil. Like Jesus' brothers, you can come and go as you please. However, if you are willing to stand by your convictions for holiness, you'd better be prepared to take some heat. Even if you are the only one in the locker room who doesn't partake of the coarse joking, you be who you are. Even if you are the only person in the cafeteria with a Bible, you be who you are.

DAY 127

PROVERBS 10:15–18

*R*ead today's Scripture. Verses 15 and 16 are, to me, two aspects of the same truth. The righteous do live in a sort of fortified city because it is hard to bring a righteous man of integrity to calamity. A wicked man, however, would be easy to expose and bring to ruin.

Verses 17 and 18, however, stand apart. Verse 17 forces us again by the compelling power of the perfect Word of God to see that we either take instruction well, or we are not acting like godly men. Have you behaved in a way that puts you on the wrong side of verse 17? Speaking of being a man of God, don't you dare spread slander (verse 18). Instead, speak in truth, strong young man of God.

DAY 128

PROVERBS 10:19-21

A box of honey-flavored Teddy Grahams does not last long here in the Campbell house, and that's not really because of my little boys. Don't judge me. When a box comes home from the store, all of us know that its contents are precious precisely because they are rare and likely to be snatched up quickly. *Read today's text.*

This day, your words will be like Teddy Grahams in the Campbell household. That is not to say that your words will be eaten violently by the fistful, per se, but it does mean that you will speak like a Proverbs 10 man today. I know that it can be so *incredibly* tempting to get the last word in, or make some obscure thought known, or impress someone with what you read on Google eight years ago, or even just let out that sentence that is ramming against the backsides of your teeth to get out, but *hold your tongue.*

DAY 129

PROVERBS 10:22

Read today's verse. The blessing described in verse 22 is a blessing precisely because you didn't have to work for it. Do you remember Adam's curse way back in the Garden of Eden in Genesis 3:17–19? As we would work our tails off together mending the fences around the horse pastures, repairing the barn, and mowing the eight acres my parents lived on, my dad would say to me over sweet tea breaks, "We are men, and these are the things men do." If you don't have to toil for something, it's a blessing from God. Would you take a moment now to run an inventory of the things in your life for which you did not have to toil? Yes, the dog counts as something for which you did not have to toil.

Do you see how blessed you are? Begin this day with a heart that drips gratitude for the little things you pass by or even step on without noticing. You are blessed, my student!

DAY 130

1 PETER 1:6–7

A man's faith is proven genuine in only one way, and that is testing it through fire. I want to speak with you directly about that one painful trial in your life. No, not the surface-level thing that doesn't actually bother you that much. I want you to go *there* to the one place in your heart that you keep tightly locked away. That experience was intended to result in praise, glory, and honor for Jesus, and it cannot possibly do so locked away like that. It's time to open long-shut doors in your heart. *Read today's Scripture.*

Just as we did when we studied James 2, we greatly rejoice today. We rejoice because through His strength, not ours, we have what it takes to withstand a testing of our faith. One of my tests was the day I was able to praise God while standing over my son's grave. What is it that is rocking your faith? Could you tell me about it face-to-face without feeling like a wuss? This trial is a testing of your faith. *Pass this test, man of God.*

DAY 131

1 PETER 1:8–9

The trials in your life serve a purpose. First of all, put them in perspective compared to the trials of other people around the world. Consider the guy who is exactly your age living in Ethiopia who will, despite his own malnourishment and dehydration, bury his mother's emaciated body today. Next, put your trials in the bigger picture of your life's story. Zoom out and see the unseen God refining your faith, making you more like Him, using you to bring others from an eternity in hell to an eternity in heaven, and then ultimately a beautiful and perfect eternity in heaven. Ah, suddenly that vocab test score doesn't seem like a big deal at all, does it? Good. Now, buck up and *read today's text*.

It does not matter what you are facing. Be filled with inexpressible and glorious joy because your soul is saved!

Day 132

1 Peter 1:10–12

Did you realize that most of human history so far has taken place *before* the life of Jesus? Generations upon generations of Jewish scholars before Jesus' time looked intently into the Scriptures to figure out the timing of the arrival of the unnamed Messiah who would take upon Himself the sins of the world. Do you remember the wise men (or "Magi") from the story of Christmas, who came bearing gifts of gold, frankincense, myrrh, and Xbox games for young Jesus? They were just a few of those scholars looking for the birth of the Messiah.

We've only just begun the third millennium since the resurrection of Jesus, but there were several more millennia before that, even in the youngest of young earth theories. Throughout all of human history, the way that man might be saved was a huge mystery, and even angels were scratching their perfect heads to see how God would bring things together. *Read today's text.*

Thousands of believers went their whole lives aching to know what you know: the name of Jesus. Take a moment to thank God that you were born into the new covenant.

DAY 133

JOHN 7:12–13

Any part of you that is afraid of being rejected by others for standing up for Jesus has to go. Either Jesus is Lord in your life, or He isn't. Don't let what others think of you keep you from being who you are. If we deny Jesus before men, He will deny us before the Father (Matthew 10:33). *Read today's text.*

Talk publicly about Jesus today. Be the bull-headed one who testifies boldly about Christ and then lets the statement sit in deliberately awkward silence as if to say, "Deal with *that*." Step out of line and misbehave. The cool thing about breaking free from what others think of you is that, if it's done in a godly way, it makes many others respect you more and want to follow you. I know I would.

DAY 134

JOHN 7:14–18

I ache with envy for those who got the chance to physically see and hear Jesus speak. When Jesus spoke, something amazing happened: God the Father spoke directly to all who were present. Rabbis of Jesus' era would sit in front of a crowd and speak by referring to the authority of other rabbis who had gone before them in the same way that students today have to cite their sources in research papers with footnotes, parenthetical citations, and bibliographies. Jesus, however, would speak with authority on direct behalf of Yahweh—no references, just perfect words. No one had ever seen such a thing. *Read today's text.*

You can speak these perfect words on behalf of Jesus now. You can reenact this amazing scene right there at the table with your friends by just weaving Scripture straight into your speech. The cool thing about speaking words on behalf of God is that, if someone doesn't like what you have to say, then he should take that up with God!

DAY 135

JOHN 7:19–24

Do you remember way back, like, thirty-two years ago in this devotional book (that may be an overestimation) when we saw Jesus heal a paralyzed man? Ever since then, the Pharisees and other Jewish leaders have been looking for an opportunity to arrest Jesus, but not because He healed a man. No, with their actions they fully testify that Jesus performed a miracle, but they want to *arrest Him* because He healed a man on the Sabbath, a day meant for rest. *Read today's text.*

Jesus uses the example that, in order to fulfill the command in Leviticus 12:3, you sometimes have to work on the Sabbath. Jesus was absolutely right, and they didn't like it, as you'll see later in John 7. These Jewish leaders were more concerned about appearing to rest on the Sabbath so that they would look righteous, and they wanted people to think that they were coming after Jesus for righteous reasons. They were *all* about appearances and not at all about heart.

In verse 24, Jesus directly gives you your challenge for the day.

DAY 136

PROVERBS 10:23-25

I have a confession to make. When I played video games as a teenager . . . *sigh* . . . I used cheat codes. Yes, I know that I just lost the respect of the hard-core, purist gamer types, but video games were way more fun with them. I loved cheat codes! They were made by the creators of the game and give the player ridiculous advantages. I know that video game cheat codes are petty, but they still paint a really cool picture of the advantages of scriptural wisdom. *Read today's text.*

I want you to *crave* spiritual wisdom from the Bible. I want you to love it, and I know that you will if you see it for what it is: a cheat code given to you by the Creator of the game. I want you to take pleasure in gaining wisdom. You'll see that, as verses 24 and 25 state, you will be secure in the whirlwinds that destroy others. You will be given what you desire that aligns with God's will.

DAY 137

PROVERBS 10:26

As I've shared before, my dad always said to me, "We are men, and these are the things men do." That phrase always accompanied doing incredibly difficult, unpleasant, dangerous, and necessary things—things that were honorable and helped the women in our family. It took years for me to overcome my slacker tendencies, but when I did, I knew then that I was a man. *Read today's text.*

As someone who works with young people, I'm usually defensive when movies, TV, and adult culture in general paint them as stupid and useless. When it comes to the stigma that teenagers tend to be slackers, though, there is not much I can do. So, think of this as a great way to stand out among your peers and do so in a way that brings glory to God. Instead of being like vinegar to his teeth and smoke to his eyes, strive today to be a blessing to the one who asks you to do something.

DAY 138

PROVERBS 10:27–30

Strong men of God obey God's commands not only because God simply says so, but also because life is just better God's way. Relationships are better God's way. Money is handled better God's way. Sex is better in marriage, which is God's way. Although the fact that these commands come from God should be more than enough reason for you to obey them, you should also obey God's commands for the long life, joy, and honor they bring. *Read today's text.*

You may be the only one of your friends who obeys God's Word, and that may isolate you at times, but I want you to know that I am proud of you and that obedience to God's Word is never in vain and never goes unrewarded. Stay the course, though at times you stay it alone.

DAY 139

1 PETER 1:13–14

Read today's Scripture. When Peter told these original readers seriously to set their minds for action, he was telling people—whose brothers and sisters in Christ were being murdered by their government—to do something incredibly dangerous. He called them to set their hope *completely* on the grace brought to them by what Jesus reveals. He called their ways of thinking and life before salvation "ignorance" and instructed them (and, in turn, you and me) to not conform to those old desires.

Our hope is not in a good football season, the promise of a new car, getting the girl, or even a degree. Our hope is, as the Word says here, *completely* on Christ, and that is great news because football teams lose, cars break down, girls sometimes go crazy, and some college degrees turn out to have been pointless. Instead, set your hope on heaven and know that, though everything else falls apart and life is unfair, you will spend eternity with God if you are saved.

DAY 140

1 PETER 1:15–16

What does it mean to be a man of holiness? It means to be set apart, striving for repentance, quick to get back up when you fall into sin, disciplined in mind when it comes to the study of God's Word, compassionate and therefore evangelistically active, and consumed with zeal (sort of like what you feel when you drink too much caffeine) for the worship of God. *Read today's text.*

A life of holiness is going out of style among Christians today. We don't hear too many calls to be holy, but we see plenty of efforts to be relevant. Even ministers sometimes prioritize looking attractive to the outside world over holiness and back away from calling people to be holy because they don't want to scare people off or offend them or seem legalistic. Forget that. God tells us to be holy, and He does so from a worthy state of integrity and authority to do so because He is holy. Be holy, man of God.

DAY 141

1 PETER 1:17–21

Have your Andrew and Philip been receptive to your invitations to church? Have you been faithful in praying for them? If not, try again today. Take a minute right now to pray the way the book of James taught to us pray when we ask God for wisdom, and that is *believing* as you ask for it. Ask God for wisdom as to how you should invite Andrew and Philip to church, or for the best way to bring up the gospel, and prepare yourself to bring up the gospel *today*.

Read today's text. Did you notice verse 17's use of "temporary residence" (in the HCSB)? That's because this earth is just a temporary home, and while we live here we are to conduct ourselves in a way worthy of the perfect sacrifice of Jesus. Ask yourself today, "Is this behavior *worthy* of Jesus' sacrifice?" That is what it looks like to conduct yourself in reverence of the Lord (verse 17).

DAY 142

JOHN 7:25–32

In some passages, we see Jesus deliberately keeping a low profile so as not to stir up the anger of the people who were after Him. In other passages, we see Him directly defying them in a really public way, and when they try to arrest Him (or push Him off a cliff in Luke 4:29), God miraculously spares Him because the time had not yet come. It makes for a fascinating dance between God's sovereign power ensuring that His will come about and God allowing man to be free to think and act wrongly. *Read today's text*.

This crowd does not know its Scripture at all. The prophecies about the Messiah *did indeed* foretell that He would be born in Bethlehem (verse 27). Unfortunately, you and I live in a very similar setting. People who have never read the Bible have strong opinions about it, and this is just the state of our culture. You, however, are the answer to that problem. Today, wait patiently for your opportunity to do exactly what Jesus does here: speak Scripture. Unless your time has come, God will protect you.

DAY 143

JOHN 7:33–36

Young man, hold fast to faith. There is hope. Today, you may be dying, but God is your redeemer. It's okay to be broken sometimes. It's okay to hurt. Being broken before your God is the place to be because He is compassionate toward you and is going to put you back together. Hold fast.

Read today's text. The Jews didn't get it. Jesus was speaking in spiritual terms, and they were thinking in earthly terms. Jesus was talking about being raised from the dead after the crucifixion, and they thought He would go teach the Greeks. Prepare to be misunderstood as a spiritual man who speaks and lives in spiritual terms. Your peers don't understand you because they don't have that spirit within them . . . at least not yet.

DAY 144

JOHN 7:37–39

Men of vision have to be willing to get up and make some noise sometimes, to make people uncomfortable in order to inspire them. Now, there is no shortage of people making noise, with social media giving anyone with fingers the chance to share something with everyone he knows, but so few are actually saying anything of importance. Jesus is about to stand up and cry out something powerful. *Read today's text.*

Get ready, because I'm about to challenge you to do something crazy. Jesus compassionately called all who are thirsty to come to Him and prophesied that the Holy Spirit would fill those who were thirsty with streams of living water. If someone is filled with streams, he is going to overflow onto everyone around him. Be filled with the Spirit in Jesus' name, my student—I'm serious about this because I've done it myself, and it was awesome—*and stand up and cry out something impactful today.* Stand up on top of your table, and let it be known that you are a Christian.

DAY 145

PROVERBS 10:31-32

Did you get up on the table yesterday? If not, try again today. I bet you'll inspire others to do the same. How cool would that be? Also, I love the idea that another strong man of God going through this same devotional might do the same thing. Ha! That would freak some people out and, who knows, may even start a powerful movement of God. No revival has ever been started by a timid man.

Speaking of speaking out, *read today's Scripture*. We have been reading from Proverbs about the value of wisdom, and in reading we have been encouraged to seek out wisdom. Today we see that we might *produce* wisdom by speaking it from hearts of righteousness. Also, righteous hearts know what is appropriate to speak and what is not. Sorry, but as funny as they are, locker-room jokes have no place on the lips of a righteous man. Speak wisdom to someone today.

PROVERBS 11:1

Be real with yourself about who you are. Be real with yourself about what you look like. Be real with how smart and cool you actually are, not what you just wish you were. Face the number on the scale, breathe in deep, and own that number as you exhale. This kind of honest self-awareness delights God. *Read today's verse.*

This passage is not just some obscure description of God's preferences when it comes to weight measuring devices. No, it is a call to get real. Don't evaluate yourself as a man based on wishful thinking. Stop fantasizing and actually be the man you want to be, starting with the man you are.

DAY 147

PROVERBS 11:2

Pride. You might say it was the real original sin. It was Satan's sin before (if you can describe it in temporal terms) the earth was created, when he as an angel pridefully thought himself equal to God. It is a particularly dangerous sin because it has no scent to the one infected by it, leaves no footprints behind the one who carries it, and fogs his mirror with lies and an inaccurate self-image. Building on what we read yesterday, *read today's text*.

Did you see that? "Disgrace" follows pride. No thanks! Though it's hard to swallow, I would rather have humility because it brings wisdom. Today, you will see who among your peers is truly insecure. He will reveal it when he speaks pridefully. Sometimes, the most confident and secure man is the quietest. He doesn't need to disgrace himself with prideful speech or public failure after attempting something that is beyond him. He simply knows who he is, and he knows who God is, and therefore wisely speaks and acts from humility.

Day 148

1 Peter 1:22-25

Read today's Scripture. Real men are men of love. They love their fellow man earnestly and from the heart. Your dad may not express his love for you, and I know that kills you, but that does not mean that you are not worthy of love. It certainly does not let you off the hook when it comes to this passage's command to show love.

If your dad has let you down by not showing you love, decide right now that this family trend ends with you, that you will now rewrite your family's history and that your sons will be men of love just like you. Decide that you will, because you have been born again, love and love *earnestly* from a sincere heart that is obedient to God's truth and purified by God's grace.

1 PETER 2:1–3

Have you ever watched the show *Hoarders*? When I need motivation to clean up our house, which gets really cluttered after Austin and Asher have played, I start to watch an episode, and the whole house is cleaner than the inside of a bleach bottle before the episode ends. *Read today's text.*

People who hoard things have a hard time getting rid of them, and we can be the same way with our sin. Now, today *get rid of* all malice, deceit, hypocrisy, envy, and slander. Don't just put them in the garage: *get rid of them*. It's time for a *Hoarders*-style purge of sin followed by a time of getting back to the basics (verse 2) so that we may grow by it for our salvation.

Malice, by the way, is just any sort of harsh negativity you have toward others. *Deceit* is when you speak or imply untruth. *Hypocrisy* is when you don't live by the standards you profess, and *slander* is falsely slamming others.

DAY 150

1 PETER 2:4–10

As we work our way through the book of John, we will continue to see Jesus rejected. Can you relate to that? Have you been rejected by other men or women? Jesus was rejected, too, only He is actually perfect. For the next six verses, Jesus is going to be referred to as a stone that is rejected and overlooked at a construction project, but that ends up becoming the cornerstone. The cornerstone is the most important and prominent stone in a structure. It bears the weight of all the others. *Read today's Scripture.*

Verse 5 says that we are like stones being put together as a dwelling place for the Holy Spirit. This is an awesome thought also described in Ephesians 2:19–22. The lost stumble over Christ, in whom they do not believe, but you have been brought from darkness into marvelous light! Look up a recording of Chris Tomlin's song "Marvelous Light," and sing it to God now.

DAY 151

JOHN 7:40-44

When we last left our Hero, He had just prophesied that the Holy Spirit would come after His resurrection and overflow from the hearts of those who believe. Today, He is going to stir up conflict in the crowd, and though it has been well over two thousand years since He left the earth, *this exact conflict still rages among men today. Read today's Scripture.*

They didn't know that Jesus was actually from Bethlehem. They thought that He was from Galilee, but they were wrong. Who else from the first century still divides people today? It's not like you could mention the name of Attalus, a famous philosopher and writer who lived at the same time as Jesus, in mixed company and possibly find yourself in an awkward confrontation. But Jesus' name does that still today (verse 43).

Despite the conflict that it sometimes brings, speak the name of Jesus out loud today. There is such power in it, and even though it may bring awkwardness, it is more than worth it.

Day 152

John 7:45–53

It is time to check up on our goals to lead Philip and Andrew to Christ, as well as to pray for our Pharisees. It is also time to reveal the other two goals, one of which is our most ambitious goal of all. Continue to lead Philip and Andrew to Christ and pray for your Pharisees. The other two goals are: (1) bring a shy and spiritually inactive closet Christian out of his shell, and (2) see your Philip and Andrew lead someone else to Christ after they are saved themselves! When someone you've evangelized evangelizes someone else, that person's name goes in the "Peter" blank. *Read today's Scripture*.

So, the cautious, closet-Christian Nicodemus from John 3 just spoke up on Jesus' behalf! On the "Praying for These" page, write in the blank next to "My Nicodemus" the name of a timid closet Christian whom you are going to encourage out of his idleness and shame. Pray for your Nicodemus now.

DAY 153

JOHN 8:1–11

Read today's Scripture. The trap set by the Pharisees was probably to claim that Jesus lacked compassion if He would have the woman stoned, but also to frame Jesus as scripturally unsound if He refused to hold up the law of Moses and follow through with the execution. Jesus did not fall into their trap. Instead, He literally, physically stood up to them (verse 7) and publicly exposed them for their own hypocrisy. Notice that the older men leave first (verse 9), probably because they know they have lived lives with sizeable sin records, whereas the young bucks were actually prideful enough to hold on to their stones for a little longer.

Jesus has such incredible compassion, but at the same time, calls this woman to repent and stop sinning (verse 11). As odd as it seems coming from a devotional book for men, you and I are *just like the woman in this passage*. We stand accused and found guilty, but Jesus stands in our defense. Be humbly grateful today because you have been spared by God from what God's own law decrees that you deserve.

DAY 154

PROVERBS 11:3–4

People who lack integrity may get away with *so much*, and watching them do so could eat you up inside. Instead, know that your integrity guides and protects you. *Read today's Scripture.*

Those who are treacherous because they scheme, plot, whisper, and lie, will eventually be destroyed by the monsters they have created. Even though they grow to be incredibly wealthy, that wealth will do nothing for them as they stand in judgment before the God who owns all things and whose wrath is against treacherous sins. So, let the wicked be wealthy. Let the treacherous succeed in their schemes. You, strong young man of God, will be the same person when in full public view as you are when no one is looking. That is what it means to be a man of integrity (verse 3).

DAY 155

PROVERBS 11:5–11

Read today's text. Obeying God's laws may be difficult, but life is *still* easier for the righteous man than it is for the wicked man. The theme among these verses about the righteous man is that he has been *rescued*. What an appropriate way to describe each and every Christian, huh? Rescued indeed. These verses speak to a sense of legacy. Which will yours be? How will people describe you after you die?

In today's text, we see a righteous man rescued by his own righteousness and by the favor of God Almighty. We see him become a blessing to an entire city and bless it with his own uprightness, but the wicked man falls, is trapped, vanishes, and is troubled. He destroys his neighbor; he tears down a city with his words, and ultimately people rejoice in his death in just seven short verses. May your legacy be that of a righteous man, and may your legacy be substantiated (meaning made true and reliable) by your conduct today. Today, live your life with your legacy in mind.

DAY 156

1 PETER 2:11–17

There may seem like two separate messages within these verses, but verses 13–17 will give you the practical advice for obeying verses 11 and 12. *Read today's text.*

So, your conduct alone can cause people to glorify God even if they do take some cheap shots at you (verse 12). Part of the way you bring that about is abiding by the law (verses 13–14), doing good that silences fools (verse 15), respecting others, loving the church, fearing God, and honoring the "emperor." This side of heaven, you will never know the impact that your upright life will have on the lost. One of the guys who gave me all sorts of grief for not drinking as a freshman in college (when *both* of us were underage) actually respected me for withstanding the peer pressure. Today he lives in Kenya, sharing the gospel with orphans.

Let your airtight testimony set your evangelistic endeavors up for success.

DAY 157

1 PETER 2:18–25

Some slavery in the Roman Empire at this time was similar to the slavery in early American history, but people of all races could be slaves. These slaves were often educated, paid, and eventually freed after a certain amount of time. At first, they had no legal rights, but for much of the Roman Empire's history, they could press charges against their own masters and even claim legal ownership over the master's property, using it as their own. Slaves were often fiercely loyal. *Read today's Scripture.*

The point of this passage is that God applauds you for standing up under unjust suffering and that facing unjust suffering gives us a glimpse of what Christ endured for us. To keep your faith, your testimony, your countenance, and your integrity intact in the midst of unjust suffering is to be like Jesus as He endured the crucifixion. Be grateful that your undeserved sufferings (not suffering the consequences of dumb decisions, but *unjust* sufferings) offer you the chance to gain the favor of God and to be like Jesus! Let not your suffering be wasted, young man.

1 Peter 3:1-6

If you are of age to begin dating for marriage, put the video games down and get a date, man. Scour the worship center, and let your eyes fixate on the woman who goes through two pens in each sermon as she takes notes. Pop a mint, and get her number like a boss. Walk past the girl who was staring at her mirror the whole time as you do. *Read today's text.*

That's the one for whom you're looking, that holy woman of God. Go get her, and treat her like an absolute princess. One of the strongest indicators that my wife was the woman I was to marry was the fact that she would show up to worship driving her mom's massive SUV, and seven Asian exchange students would pile out with her. Now, about this submission thing (verse 1), you keep in mind that you are called in Ephesians 5:25–30 to give up your life for your wife in the way Christ did for the church. A woman has no problem submitting to the leadership of a man who would endure an unjust crucifixion for her. With that in mind, *go hunt.*

DAY 159

JOHN 8:12–20

Read today's text. The treasury in the temple complex, which according to verse 20 is where Jesus spoke these bold words, was a prominent and public place. So, a huge crowd of onlookers certainly saw Jesus defy the Pharisees outright and then *not* get arrested afterward. Although the Pharisees and Jesus go back and forth as they have done before, that debate illustrates what Jesus said in verse 12. These Pharisees are in the dark, and their immediate protest shows it. They never understand Jesus' teachings because they are in the dark, the dark of legalism (meaning they cared more about obeying rules than having a relationship with God) and the dark of lost-ness, as they didn't have the light of life that comes from following Jesus.

This world is full of such darkness, but Jesus is the light. I have been all over the world and have seen the darkness of poverty, abandonment, depression, grief, abuse, and even demonic stuff. Jesus is the light that overcomes all of that darkness. Light up the darkness. Be a man of God among Pharisees, and pray that they would see the light of life. Pray *hard* for your Pharisees.

DAY 160

JOHN 8:21–29

Hell is biblical and real. Let's be men about this. There are people who will go to hell today because they will die without believing that Jesus is Lord. I know that's gargantuanly unpleasant. I know it's not something people talk about, but it is the truth. *Read today's text.*

This is more of the same from the Pharisees, but I want you to focus in on what Jesus says in verse 24 because it is, like everything else Jesus says, true. Take a deep breath and deal with the weight of that verse if you can. Do not let grief overwhelm you. Instead, let the immense severity of hell push you out of your insecurity in talking with others about Christ and doing so *today*. If you believe what Jesus said in verse 24, how could you let this school year end without at least bringing up the gospel? See the previous devotional for practical instructions on exactly what you need to do.

JOHN 8:30–36

Start by reading only the *first verse*, please. In light of the past two devotionals, doesn't that sound amazing? Let your imagination run with the vision of what it would look like to see many people believe in Jesus as you say these things. Knowing that someone's eternity is at stake in evangelism, the thought of revival breaking out fills me with a sense of simultaneous ecstasy and relief. *Now, read the rest, please.*

Let it be said of you that you continue in Jesus' words so that you really are His disciple. Though most are slaves to sin, you are free and free indeed! Don't you love how He threw that "you really will be free" (verse 36) in to drive the point home? You are not just free from sin; you really are free! Now, live like it! In the name of Jesus, I dispel the lie that Satan has put over you saying that you cannot get rid of that particular sin, whatever it may be. *No!* You are really and truly free!

DAY 162

PROVERBS 11:12–13

Part of being a man is being trustworthy, trustworthy to get a job done and trustworthy to keep private that which your brother shares with you. *Read today's Scripture.*

These two sets of couplets are next to one another for a reason. I wonder if the neighbor in the first part of verse 12 sort of deserved to get slammed for whatever he did. Either way, a man with understanding keeps silent. That can be tough: to have a fully justifiable case to bring the hammer down on someone, but keeping silent instead. If you can show enough self-control to keep verse-12 silence, then you are verse-13 trustworthy. Though your neighbor (not necessarily the one who makes awesome cookies, but anyone you see today) might be acting in a way that is worthy of contempt, you are going to keep silent and thereby prove that you are worthy of someone's confidence.

Day 163

Proverbs 11:14–20

*R*ead today's Scripture. All of these verses are amazing, but verse 14 is one of my favorite proverbs.

Verse 14 calls for a pretty exciting possible change in your life. You need a team of advisors. If he's in the picture and has his act together, I nominate your dad for your first-round draft pick. Do you have an older brother who isn't a cannibal? Consider him as well. I suggest family because they are going to be there for you your whole life if they can. I'm married with kids, but I spoke with both my dad and my brother today for advice, as I've been doing all my life. Write down the names of your potential advisors and draft them to your team before the sun sets.

DAY 164

PROVERBS 11:21

In the movies, the good guys win, and the bad guys get what's coming to them, right? But in the movie of your life, you're not all that good of a good guy when you get right down to it. *Read today's text.*

Verse 21 is a reminder that those who live wicked lives, though they might get away with it (or at least appear to get away with it) for now, they have theirs coming. Don't be tempted to follow their paths. Believe me: you don't want what's at the end of it. Also, did you notice the deliberate wording of this verse to say that the righteous will "escape"? Because of our sin, our righteousness is like polluted garments before God (Isaiah 64:6). Our sin makes us worthy of hell, but the grace of God allows us to, as today's proverb states, "escape." So, there is no room for ego here, righteous guy. It's not that you don't have sin like the other guy: it's that you will escape eternal separation from God because of what Jesus has done for you.

DAY 165

1 PETER 3:7

Though you may be years away from getting married, it is *not* too early to start preparing for marriage. It's time to start thinking like a husband. *Read today's verse.*

In the original Greek text of this verse, the wife is described as the more delicate vessel (*asthenestero skeuei*) than the man. She is depicted as priceless fine china, and that is why she is to be handled delicately. That is why she is to be honored. Now, *read the last part of this verse again.* What happens when you fail to treat her like delicate fine china and honor her because she is a fellow recipient of God's grace of life? Your prayers are hindered! Just imagine not learning this verse until after marriage! Whew, it's a good thing you bought this book and read that verse. Do you see why it's not too early to start preparing for marriage by thinking like a husband?

DAY 166

1 PETER 3:8–12

The original recipients of this top-secret letter lived in an incredibly hostile region and were top-secret teammates in evangelism. They needed to be like-minded, loving, and forgiving toward one another, because when they evangelized, they risked their lives! Americans today evangelize at the risk of an awkward social encounter. *Read today's text.*

Verses 8 and 9 should describe your heart toward your church and fellow believers. If no one else at your church is being compassionate and humble and gracious, then *you step up and be the first.* Others will follow. Also, did you notice all of the different parts of the human face as well as God's face that are named in verses 10–12? Fascinating. Face-to-face.

1 PETER 3:13–17

As we prayed that our son Aiden would live and publicly asked people to pray through Facebook, my many atheist friends took notice, and I got the chance to see many of them come to Christ! I was ready to give them an answer for the hope I had despite all the odds against my baby boy. *Read today's text.*

So, you need to be ready. I have put together a pretty good resource for learning how to prove God's existence. It can also be handed directly to someone who does not believe in God or those who just sort of believe. It's entitled "Faith & Reason," and it is available for download from the ARTICLES page of my website.

Now, keep verse 16 in mind as you share! You have to have integrity so that those who slam you will be shamed for it, and you have to share this in a way that is super respectful, so that people are more likely to hear what you have to say. There are plenty of other awesome resources to help you back up your faith with reason. Go study apologetics! Be prepared!

Day 168

John 8:37–59
(Yep, this one's a bigger passage.)

We have been looking at the Bible with a microscope, mostly in small portions of Scripture at a time, but I want you to zoom out a little today so that you can see something beautifully intricate and brilliantly designed in this chapter. It's called a chiastic structure (pronounced emphasizing the *ki* as in "kite"—*kiastick*), and it is a passage that shows or talks about a series of events or ideas and then revisits those same events and ideas in reverse order as in the sequence "ABCDCBA." John 8 moves from a thwarted stone throwing to "I am" to fathers to demon possession and quickly back again to end with another thwarted stoning. *Read today's text.*

We tend to do what our fathers want us to do, so we tend to be like our fathers. Sometimes, that is a great thing, but other times it's horrible. Let it be known by your belief in Jesus and your godly lifestyle that you are a child of God (John 1:12). If your earthly father has just completely let your family down, I want you to know that God your heavenly Father can adopt you and affirm you in your masculinity.

DAY 169

JOHN 9:1–7

A quick note about our last devotional: when Jesus says "I am" in verse 58, He is aligning Himself directly with the name with which God introduced Himself to Moses. So, in this passage, the great I AM is about to perform a beautiful miracle. *Read today's text.*

Like this man's lifelong blindness, sometimes our afflictions (again, not the consequences of our own poor choices, but our afflictions) serve a beautiful purpose: that God would use them to make His glory known (verse 3). Take that truth and press it hard against the afflictions in your life. It is possible that God allowed this to happen just so that He could bring you through it for all to see (see next devotional). Also, let this blind man's story in these seven verses tell the story of your own Philip and Andrew, who, like all of us, were born blind in sin, but then met Jesus and took steps of faith (blind faith to be exact) in obedience to Jesus and told them, "Go, wash in the pool of Siloam (which means sent)" and walk away seeing! They once were blind, but now, in the name of Jesus, let them see!

DAY 170

2 CORINTHIANS 12:6–10

Building on the previous devotional, what happens when God doesn't deliver us from affliction? Is it because we lack faith? No, though everyone who is healed of God has faith, not everyone who has faith is healed. *Sometimes, it is God's will that you be afflicted.*

Read today's Scripture. There are some things that only come about through affliction. Paul was an awesome man of God, an apostle, and the author of much of the New Testament, yet God did *not* deliver him from his afflictions, though he prayed repeatedly in faith for deliverance. God allowed that affliction upon Paul because God wanted to achieve something beautiful through it. Here's another example: Jesus actually prayed to be spared the crucifixion in Luke 22:42 and then ended by saying, "nevertheless, not My will, but Yours be done." It was God's will that Jesus be afflicted, and through that affliction He brought about salvation for all who believe. There are some things, beautiful things, that only come about through affliction. Welcome that kind of affliction in your life.

DAY 171

JOHN 9:8–12

I pray that by now you have been bold enough to have shared your faith with Andrew and Philip and that, in Jesus' name, you have been a part of the harvest and seen someone saved! If not, *get on it*. Now, the most effective thing that will help bring about Peter (that is the one whom Andrew introduced to Jesus after Andrew was introduced by John the Baptist) is the radical transformation in Andrew's or Philip's life. A testimony of transformation will make waves. *Read today's text*.

People didn't recognize the man who had been born blind. Again, his story runs so beautifully parallel to that of someone who is being saved. Coach this new Christian to live his testimony out loud. Peter is watching, and I'll bet you have an idea who he is!

DAY 172

PROVERBS 11:22

This is probably the funniest of all the Proverbs. *Read today's text.*

Ha! I don't care who you are; that's funny. The girl is the pig, and her beauty is the ring. Let that gold ring shine: it's still stuck in a pig's snout. Let that girl look like a model: she still lacks discretion, and that makes her . . . the pig in this verse. Bahaha!

My student, you cannot help but first be attracted to a woman's looks based on the fact that your eyes have a greater range than that of your other sensory faculties. Men who do not prioritize holiness the way you do need nothing more than their sense of sight to determine if a woman is a worthy recipient of their affections, but your standards are different. What makes a woman worthy of pursuit is her godly character. Looks, though they are important to an extent, are not to surpass godly character on your list of desirable traits in a woman.

175

Day 173

Proverbs 11:23–31

This morning, my wife told me that we were late getting our tithe (one-tenth of our income) to the church, and that we suddenly had several unexpected expenses. Usually, when we pay our tithe, we receive the same amount back in other opportunities, like last-minute drumming gigs or speaking engagements. God promised to open the floodgates of heaven with uncontainable blessings in Malachi 3:10, and He promised it so that our hearts would be after His church and His kingdom more than after worldly things. Where you spend your money is the mathematically certain indicator of where your heart is. *Read today's text.*

Trust in God instead of riches (verse 28), give freely and you may gain back more (verse 24), and be a generous person today (verse 25), thus obeying the wisdom of God.

PROVERBS 12:1–3

Our first verse of the day contains a word my three-year-old, Austin, isn't allowed to say. Ha! *Read today's text.*

Wow. I think you may have just sped past something that you need to savor a little longer to appreciate. Think. about. having. God's. *FAVOR.* We work hard to have the coach's favor, but what about obtaining the favor of the one who spoke the stars into existence? Oh, to be established in righteousness so that you cannot be uprooted . . . to be favored by the One who designed Saturn's rings. Sorry, what were you desiring before you had this devotional? It does not compare to that.

Now, what does that require? It requires good, godly conduct (verse 2) and loving discipline (verse 1). That's right: *loving* discipline. Cherish correction! Have the maturity to see beyond the discipline or correction itself, and focus on what that discipline produces.

1 PETER 3:18–20

This is insane: Jesus got all up in some demons' faces and told them what was up! *Read today's text.*

These are the same demons that were messing around when Noah was building the ark, and Jesus—after being put physically to death, but spiritually just as alive as ever after the crucifixion—made the bold proclamation to their faces that He was victorious and would bring you to God. Right now, let all the special effects you've seen in movies actually do you some good, and just imagine that scene playing out like a movie in your head. Amazing, right? Jesus is victorious over demons. In fact, they are terrified of Him. Take a peek at Mark 5:11–13 and see that demons would rather literally inhabit suicidal pigs than be near Jesus. Don't get freaked out over demons. Instead, let them be terrified of Jesus, who lives within you.

DAY 176

1 PETER 3:20–22

(Reread verse 20 from yesterday, please.)

There is something else here as well. Not only does this passage lay out how victorious and dominating Jesus is over the same ancient demons that have been around for millennia (verse 22), but it also shows these amazing parallels between the water of the flood and the water in which we are baptized. *Read today's text.*

The flood was God's coming wrath upon sin, of which He warned people and warned people and warned them, but they mocked God's prophet Noah (my son Asher's middle name; we have a thing for Old Testament prophets). So in the same way that the floodwaters washed away the blasphemous sin of the world, the waters of baptism symbolize the washing away of our sin, of dying and rising to live as a new creation. If you have not been baptized, *be baptized already*, you procrastinator. It is a beautiful, worshipful, inspiring metaphor that depicts the cleansing power that Jesus' resurrection has in those who believe.

DAY 177

1 PETER 4:1–6

Put on your big-Christian pants. This is a controversial passage. It has been used in the past to teach that people have a second shot at accepting Christ after they die. Such a grave misinterpretation—hear me, my student—*is exactly what Satan wants the world to believe.* We are about to get our Greek on. *Read today's text.*

Did you notice how the language of verse 4 built upon the last two devotions' teachings? Those swept away in the flood mocked those on the ark but will have to explain this to God, and their explanations will fall short because, according to verse 6, they had the chance to respond to the gospel when they were alive. We know this because, if verse 6 is referring to the same people that the end of chapter 3 was referring to, they had the gospel repeated to them over and over again by Noah. The words "was . . . preached" in verse 6 are in what's called the "aorist" tense in Greek, meaning these people had their chance in the past.

You're smart enough and strong enough to realize what this means for your lost friends. *Evangelize, Noah.*

DAY 178

JOHN 9:13–17

The healing of the man born blind has to be the grossest of Jesus' miracles. Imagine the curious crowd riveted with rapturous anticipation as Jesus approached him. Would He create two twin whirlwinds of light, one for each of the man's eyes? Would He cause the man to levitate and then have two archangels appear and touch the man's impotent eye sockets? Would He—

Right about that time, Jesus hocks a big one right into the dirt, smears the spit-made mud smack on the guy's eyes, and tells him to go wash it off.

Well . . . tha' . . . wasn't how . . . I jus' . . . I pictured that going differently, the crowd thinks.

Think hard about what it means that the man had to go wash to be healed. Get this, my student: this man never saw Jesus, though Jesus healed him. *Read today's text.* Did you notice that, in verse 17, the man simply called Jesus a prophet when Jesus was so much more than that? Remember that for later. For now, though, think on how beautiful it is that, although you have never seen Jesus, Jesus has healed you. Reread 1 Peter 1:8–9.

DAY 179

JOHN 9:18–23

The Pharisees are at it again. They are trying so hard to prove that Jesus worked on the Sabbath, when all Jesus did was spit! They do not believe that Jesus actually healed the man born blind until they hear it from the man's parents. *Read today's text.*

This poor guy was hung out to dry by his parents in front of his accusers. They forsook their own son publicly just so that they would not be kicked out of the synagogue. Are your parents not believers in Christ? I hope you will show them grace. Are you afraid of the rejection that comes from being associated with Jesus? I hope that you will not forsake the Son of God for the opinions of men.

DAY 180

JOHN 9:24–34

You may not have a fully working understanding of all things theological just yet, and that's okay. You may not understand amillennialism, dispensationalism, Arminianism, or any other -ism just yet, and though it is a good thing to study the deep stuff, you don't need them in order to be saved. The man born blind could not explain how he was healed. All he knew was that he was blind but could now see. *Read today's text.*

I wonder if this guy wished he couldn't see after all on this terrible day. It seems that a lifetime of speaking without being able to see how words affected people gave him a sense of candor and fearlessness in speech. Also, note verse 34. The religious leaders plotting the illegal murder of a miracle worker told the man testifying the truth about the Messiah that he was "born entirely in sin" and kicked him out. I want you to be like this healed man today. Own the fact that you don't *yet* have all the answers, but know at least that you can see now. Let the Pharisees condemn you for it. In condemning you as a sinner, they doubly condemn themselves.

DAY 181

PROVERBS 12:4

Before I began to type this passage, I just got on my face to pray. And I didn't pray for you: I prayed for your future wife. *Read today's verse.*

Don't let this threat of bone rot make you think that "choosing the wrong wife" will ruin you because, in a sense, they're all "the wrong wife." They all have sin. Resolve that you will find a capable wife of quality and godly character. If in marriage you one day think that you have married the wrong wife, you will treat her as though she *were* a Proverbs 12:4 wife. Then, she will *become* your Proverbs 12:4 wife. Don't chase the adulterous woman. Chase the godly woman. Chase the Proverbs 12:4 girl, and for the sake of your bones, forsake all the others, no matter how pretty they may be.

Day 182

Proverbs 12:5–8

Today, you will focus on refining your thoughts and speech that they might be those of a strong man of God. *Read today's Scripture.*

Let your thoughts, in accordance with this Scripture today, be not self-serving, but just. Let your words today be not misleading, but upright. Verses 5 and 6 describe such thoughts and speech, while verses 7 and 8 describe their end result. Look at those end results one more time by rereading verses 7 and 8. Do you want that? *Yeah, you do!* You aspire to be praised for your insight, and you determine now that your house will stand while the wicked man's falls. You do that by taking captive your every thought today and making it obedient to Christ (2 Corinthians 10:5), then speaking accordingly.

Day 183

Proverbs 12:9–12

As the future provider for a family, it's important that you begin to think like a provider. Today's text is all about being for real (verse 9) and working hard (verse 11). *Read today's text.*

Security is incredibly important to a woman, so to be desired by the kind of woman you desire (and that is a godly one), you also need to be an able provider one day. Several of your buddies will likely be Peter Pans, but *not you.* They will, like the other guy in verse 11, chase fantasies.

Now, this is coming from a guy who has a degree in drumming, but I do actually make money from that and even owned a profitable small business specializing in it. By all means, as you plan your future career, think about what you love. Also, think about whom you love . . . and how she might like to eat something besides Ramen noodles every night.

DAY 184

1 PETER 4:7–11

Today, you think about what kind of church member you are. The members of this church in Rome in AD 64 were being persecuted like crazy. When someone would show up late for his designated arrival time to Bible study in the catacombs, the church would think he may have been caught and captured. Of all the things that Peter could have told these Christians to do (self-defense classes, how to overthrow the government, how to perform miracles), he tells them above all else to love one another. *Read today's text.*

Too many young men think of the church as a place that exists to entertain, engage, and serve them, when the *opposite* is true. Turn that notion on its head. You go to church to be equipped from God's Word, to worship with God's people, and to love every person who walks in the door (verse 8). This love covers a multitude of wrongs, and that's good because there is always a multitude of wrongs at every church. So, what kind of church member are you? I hope you're a strong man of God who serves his church, because the churches I know desperately need more of those.

Day 185

1 Peter 4:12–19

Don't take this the wrong way, but I hope you suffer today. Haha! *Read today's text.*

I hope you suffer because those who suffer for bearing the name of Christ and for doing good are blessed by God. Suffer rejection and consider it an honor that you bear the name "*Christ*-ian" because in that suffering you are sharing in what Christ endured (verse 13). Just as verse 19 instructs, you continue to do good and entrust yourself to your Creator because, as you suffer, *He is faithful still.*

Your sufferings as a Christian (provided that they came about because you acted like Christ) are verification that you are on the right track. On the other side of that fact is an uncomfortable truth: if you have never suffered at all for your Christian faith, it may mean that you are not living a life like Christ's. The silence of non-Christians around you might speak a message that is just as loud as a persecutor's shout.

Day 186

1 Peter 5:1–5

My big brother always plowed the trail for me and to this day still gives me advice from a life that is eight years ahead of mine. My dad, of course, mentored me, but that was a different type of mentorship because he was authoritative over me, whereas my brother was not. Growing up, I was so grateful for it that I began to mentor some of the middle-school guys in my youth group when I was a high-school student. Then, I saw just how much of a blessing it is to mentor younger guys: it's more of a blessing than being mentored. *Read today's text.*

The idea of an elder is God's design for this kind of mentoring and protecting, but applied specifically to the church. Pray right now, as the faces of the younger guys in your church pass through your mind, that God would reveal to you the one whom you are to take under your wing. You'll find accountability, discipline, an investment of joy, and a harvest of spiritual fruit if you do.

DAY 187

JOHN 9:35–41

*R*ead today's passage. This is the first time that the man born blind *sees* Jesus (verse 37)! Likewise, you and I have been healed of our sin by Jesus (if you are saved), but we will not see Him until we are in heaven. *I can hardly wait until that day!* Take a couple of minutes right now and just try to imagine the coming reunion with your Healer.

Now, did you notice that Jesus' statement in verse 39 came true in verses 35–41? The man who was blind saw in verses 35–38. Then, the Pharisees who saw the Word of God proved themselves to be blind in verses 40 and 41.

DAY 188

JOHN 10:1–10

I hope that you have such a close relationship with the Good Shepherd that you recognize His voice when He speaks to you. *Read today's text*.

Jesus was preceded and followed by people who claimed to be the Messiah, but these were false shepherds. They were thieves, and the thief in this metaphor represents Satan. He comes to steal your sense of masculinity, kill your effectiveness as a man, and destroy what your masculinity has accomplished. Jesus, however, came that we may have life *and have it abundantly*. Do you remember how He filled those stone jars with wine? He filled them to the brim and wants to fill you with abundant life. Today, be watchful of that which would steal, kill, and destroy because it is influenced by and working toward the mission of (verse 10) Satan.

DAY 189

JOHN 10:11–21

It takes one dedicated shepherd to lay down his life for a bunch of smelly and even disloyal sheep. *Read today's text.*

That is exactly the kind of Shepherd Jesus is. He laid down His life for you. Press that truth hard against your heart right now. It's easy for people who have heard that over and over again to just let it pass them by, but this is no mere cliché. It is a powerful truth, and you need to understand its ramifications. Furthermore, look at what verse 18 reveals about Jesus' conduct while on the cross. He was there by His own will to carry out the Father's command. It was not the nails that kept Jesus on the cross: *it was Jesus.*

DAY 190

PROVERBS 12:13–19

*R*ead today's text. The evil man is *trapped* by his own words. Have you ever been stuck covering up a lie? Your own words trap you when you speak rebelliously (verse 13). Also, did you notice verse 15 and how it almost seems not to fit? The other six verses in today's passage pertain to speech, but this one pertains to listening. It is not there by accident; the wise man who speaks truthfully does so because he listens to good advice.

Verse 18 is a prophecy, and you will watch for it to come true today. When someone speaks rashly and ends up hurting someone as a result, listen (verse 15) to this biblical and therefore good advice: your words will bring healing to that person after the damage has been done by the one who speaks without thinking.

DAY 191

PROVERBS 12:20–22

The world of men can be hostile, but you will be a promoter of peace when peace can be realized. As a result, you will have joy. *Read today's text.*

Did you notice that verse 21 does *not* say that the righteous never faces disaster, but that the disaster doesn't *overcome* the righteous? Being righteous does not exempt you from catastrophe. In fact, Jesus tells us outright that we will have trouble in this life, but that He has *overcome* the world (John 16:33 NIV)! Isn't it amazing how those two verses work together? It's almost like verse 21 is both a piece of wisdom that is also a prophecy about Jesus written centuries before He came to the earth.

For me, it was a son who was born without a trachea. That was my disaster. I ache for the ability to tell you what yours will be, but I at least can warn you that even righteous men will face disaster and that those who are faithful bring God delight (verse 22). When righteous men like you face disaster, *they overcome it.*

DAY 192

PROVERBS 12:23

I cannot tell you how much I want you to really and truly master the immense wisdom in this tiny verse. If I had mastered this concept fourteen years ago, I would have way fewer foot-in-my-mouth moments and way fewer regrets. I used the word *master* twice deliberately because it is one thing to understand something, but another to have mastered it. *Read today's text.*

Memorize this verse. Someone who is truly wise and crafty will not let on just how much he knows. On many occasions, it is better to keep what you know to yourself even if an opportunity presents itself to share it. My heart was foolish in the past because I would jump on every opportunity to speak up (particularly when it was an opportunity to speak about myself and how awesome I thought I was). In time I learned that I was wrong and that the very people to whom I spoke were often more awesome than I thought I was, but were not running their mouths about it . . . which made them even *more* awesome. *Master* this concept by concealing knowledge today.

Day 193

1 Peter 5:6

God is able to spare you from all of your problems. He is able to make you succeed at everything you attempt. He is capable of keeping anything bad from ever happening to you and every person you love. He has the power to lift you up right this very second, . . . *but He doesn't always do that*, and that doesn't change a single thing about His power or goodness. *Read today's text.*

Read this and don't blink. God is the all-powerful Creator of the universe, who brought all the stars of the universe into existence *ex nihilo* just by speaking. He is *obviously* able to lift you up, but He will *not* do it until you are humble. Did you read that? I don't think you did. Read it again right now. The sovereign (meaning "in-charge") God, who knows you better than you do and who knows the future that you don't, will lift up the humble in the timing He sovereignly knows and decides is best, not just for them and their urges, but for those around them and for His sovereign purposes.

DAY 194

1 PETER 5:7

Are you broken and hurting today? Have all the troubles of your life just stacked up into this overwhelming heap that crushes your shoulders and presses down on your heart? I have devoted two devotions in a row to two single verses in a row because these two verses are two of the most important verses for young men to learn in the whole Bible. This verse applies directly to young men who are hurting. *Read today's text.*

Do you know what it means to *cast* your cares upon God? It means that they aren't on you anymore. You have cast them off, and they are now on God, who is never overwhelmed. Also, did you know that God cares about you? He cares that your heart is broken. He cares that you are overwhelmed. He cares for you. So, throw everything on Him now.

DAY 195

1 PETER 5:8–9

Today's passage is unpleasant, unsettling, and unreal, but it is necessary that you read it. *Read today's text.*

Be alert. Have your wits about you as if you would on a camping trip in the African jungle at night, when hungry lions can be heard roaring and their roars grow closer every minute, putting them within a mile of your camp. Stand firm with faith and resist the enemy. Do not just give in to temptation at its first appearance; that would be offering yourself to the lion as soon as he appears in your camp. You have already been promised victory over him and guaranteed never to be put in a fight with temptation that you cannot win (1 Corinthians 10:13). If you follow through with this verse and resist, the devil will flee from you (James 4:7). So, be prepared, huntsman.

DAY 196

JOHN 10:22-39

Speaking of bullies, Jesus faces His own in today's passage. A conniving crowd of them sit and wait to surround Jesus and gang up on Him. *Read today's text.*

I love two things about this passage, and the first is that Jesus says in verse 38, "You don't believe me, [then] believe the works [I perform]." People may not dig your Christianity, but they can't argue with the results you produce as a teammate, student, musician, or friend. The other is *extremely* important for all Christians, and that is Jesus' statement about our salvation (verse 28). Do not believe the enemy's lies: *nothing* can snatch you out of God's hand because nothing is greater than God, the One who holds your salvation.

DAY 197

JOHN 10:40–42

Even Jesus needed to get away from the crazy people sometimes. *Read today's text.*

After this tense standoff with the Pharisees, Jesus gets away from all the people who are trying to kill Him and heads back to friendly territory on the other side of the Jordan River, back where the gospel of John started. Absolutely, Jesus would engage people head-on in hostile territory, and that defined much of His ministry: casting out demons in huge numbers, directly resisting Satan himself, and even insulting the Pharisees to their faces. However, He also knew when to get away for a while. He knew when people were just wasting His time, shooting Him down no matter what, so when He got away, He spent that time where it served a purpose. Sometimes that purpose was to go and heal people or speak to a mostly friendly crowd, but other times it was just to get away (Matthew 12:15; 15:21; Luke 9:10; and John 6:15). If Jesus did it, you need to do it sometimes too. Look at what happened in verse 42: many people believed who might not have if He had stuck around with the stubborn Pharisees.

DAY 198

JOHN 11:1–27

Read today's Scripture. Do you know that one guy whom everyone just loves? That guy was Lazarus. In fact, when they told Jesus about Lazarus, they didn't even have to use his name (verse 3), and the disciples wanted to die too (verse 16). Take note of the fact that Jesus waited (verse 6), and that He knew all along that there was a God-glorifying purpose behind all of this (verse 4), even though everyone around Him was freaking out. In fact, He even speaks with direct confidence of this purpose in the face of Martha's accusation in verse 21.

Let everyone else lose faith and freak out. Today, we learn about how to be a strong man of God from a woman named Martha who knew that God could raise the dead and knew that Jesus was the Son of God, even though His prophecies (verse 4) seemed to be falling apart. Just as Jesus shows in this text, God knows how things are going to end, man. He is never caught off guard.

PROVERBS 12:24–28

Pray for your Pharisees, follow up with your Andrew and Philip so that you can finally fill in that "Peter" blank if you have not already, and get ready to encourage your Nicodemus (a closet-Christian friend) today. *Read today's Scripture.*

While verses 24 and 27 are always worth a second look in a world full of distractions for young men, our focus today will be on verses 25 and 26. You see, it's hard to be Nicodemus. The Holy Spirit is always convicting you, but the way others perceive you can seem more important, and the whole thing just produces a lot of anxiety. So, being careful in the way you deal with your neighbor (verse 26), cheer up Nicodemus today with a positive word on what he's doing right. Think about it ahead of time, and make sure that it is genuine. You'll find that encouraging others deliberately like this is just as much a blessing to you as it is to Nicodemus.

DAY 200

PROVERBS 13:1–6

The rough truth about being a slacker is that you can't ever really take a break from it. *Read today's Scripture.*

Take inventory of the negatively described man in these verses and honestly, *honestly,* see if you have demonstrated any of these attributes in the last three days: mockery, treachery, mouth-running, slacker behavior, lying, and downright wickedness. Take these behaviors before God, and do so with humble self-awareness. Take these behaviors to the cross and repent because you have been saved. Repent also because, as the passage shows, life is simply better when walked in repentance. Though being a slacker with a loud mouth may be easier at first, it is ultimately easier to respond to discipline well, to speak well, to guard your words well, to work diligently, to speak honestly, and to live honorably.

Day 201

Proverbs 13:7–19

There is a correlation between a life that adheres to discipline and a life that is blessed with wealth. The undisciplined man tries to obtain wealth without having actually done anything to earn it, and it never works out for him. Sorry, dude: that's just the way it is . . . unless your parents are loaded . . . in which case, congrats. *Read today's Scripture.*

I know that the hard work on this side of the professional man you're going to be one day can be grueling. I know that the payoff for everything you're doing now seems as though it is eons away, but it is closer than you think. The way you conduct yourself now will matter more then than you may think. Duck your head down, hold on tight to the ball, and power through this phase of life adhering to discipline, staying humble, and being completely real with people as you do. The reward is rich, even if it isn't money.

DAY 202

1 PETER 5:10–14

Congratulations! Today, you finish a pretty in-depth verse-by-verse study of another complete book of the Bible! This is a big deal, and I hope that you will hold the book of 1 Peter—along with the hard-core, outlaw Christians to whom it was originally written—close to your heart. *Read today's text.*

Your suffering will only last as long as God intends and your behavior allows, and after that comes a time of restoration (verse 10). So, as you endure suffering, you stand firm in the true grace of God, the promise of eternity to come in heaven. That grace on which you stand and the reward of heaven utterly dominate any of the sufferings this life brings. Just as the outlaw Christians in the first century under Nero's persecution did and today's underground church members do, put your hope in heaven, and let the trials you face in the meantime serve only to prove your faith fireproof.

DAY 203

JOHN 11:28-37

Have you ever said to God, "If You had been here, this terrible thing wouldn't have happened! Where were You?" If so, you aren't the first. Have you ever wondered how God feels about the tragedies in your life? It may seem obscure, but it's important to think not just about our own feelings, but to see what the Bible says about God's feelings. *Read today's text.*

First Martha and now Mary (not Jesus' mom, but Martha's sister) just brought this "if you had been here . . ." accusation before Jesus. In verse 4, Jesus prophesied that it wouldn't end in death, but Lazarus *is* dead. In verse 6, instead of coming right away, Jesus stayed where He was for two days! Is it because He didn't care? *Not at all.* In verses 35 and 36, Jesus showed how much He loved Lazarus by weeping for his death. Get this: when we weep, God weeps with us. He is not indifferent to your pain. Trust in God's perfect timing. Just as you will soon see in Lazarus's story, God has a reason for waiting to come to your rescue.

DAY 204

JOHN 11:38–44

It didn't make sense that Jesus would heal a man born blind but not raise His close friend from the dead. Jesus was weeping with those who wept. Though He was the perfect and omniscient (meaning "all-knowing") God, He was grief stricken over what had happened. In fact, He was *angry* (verse 38 HCSB). *Read today's Scripture.*

Think about what this reveals about the nature of God. He is angry for the unfair grief we have to experience in this life for the time being, but there is a day coming when He will bring the dead to life! This scene of Jesus raising Lazarus from the dead is relived every time someone is saved. God calls us by name, we rise up by belief that is verified by repentance, and then the grave clothes are to come off through what's called "sanctification."

Are you still wearing any of your burial clothes? If so, you look ridiculous, like a mummy wearing a ball cap. Today, if you've been saved, but are still wearing those grave clothes like Lazarus was, then strip the last of your unrepentance away now so that you may be let loose on the world (verse 44).

DAY 205

JOHN 11:45

Now that Lazarus has been raised from the dead, let's look back on what didn't make sense earlier. It is not until today's verse that Jesus' prophecy in verse 4 and His waiting around for two days in verse 6 make sense. *Read today's verse.*

Had Jesus learned about Lazarus's illness and immediately caught the first express camel to Judea, He would have shown up before Lazarus died, and this resurrection miracle would not have taken place. Also, these Jews who were saved after having witnessed the miracle would not have been there to see it. If you have called out to Jesus for deliverance, but He has not arrived, then trust and know that His perfect timing is setting the stage to bring the maximum amount of glory for God possible. As you wait patiently on the Lord, make your mind up right now that you will give God all the glory if and when He chooses to show up and bring a dead situation to life. Do not waste this chance to prove your faith in God's timing to be genuine. Be able to say when it is all over that you had faith all along.

DAY 206

PROVERBS 13:20–25

This collection of verses is power-packed, and the first one right out of the gate is going to challenge you heavily today. *Read today's passage.*

Bam! Not only should you see parental discipline as proof of love (verse 24) and set aside an inheritance for your grandchildren (verse 22), but you should also take a serious look at the company you keep, specifically the company that influences your wisdom and behavior (verse 20). Walk with the wise, my student. Don't be a companion to fools. Absolutely, be their friend and lead them to Christ, but don't accompany (see the root word *company* here) them in their foolish exploits. For example, you should pray for your buddies who are piling into the back of a pickup truck to torch mailboxes, not join them.

Take an honest look at the company you keep. Distance yourself from fools. Take an objective look at the guys you want to be like. Today, directly take action to associate yourself with the wise. That means send a Facebook message, walk across the room, offer the guy or guys a cup of coffee—do whatever it takes to initiate a friendship. And *do it today.* Walk with the wise.

DAY 207

PROVERBS 14:1–16

As you read these proverbs, do not feel that the one verse upon which this devotional focuses is the only one God intends for you to learn today. God's Word is perfect, and this devotional is only your tour guide through it, so please be sensitive to the Holy Spirit's leading. Focus where God leads you to focus, even if it is on a verse that this devotional overlooks for the sake of space. *Read today's Scripture.*

I'm zooming in on the hardest of these verses to interpret. Verse 4 says that if you want an abundant harvest, you have to take care of the ox and everything that goes into him . . . and out of him. If a church wants a full-time pastor, they need to pay him (1 Corinthians 9:9–14 and 1 Timothy 5:17–18). If you want a church, you have to deal with people (Colossians 3:13). Similarly, if you want to get the full scholarship, you're going to have to bust your tail. If you want the big paycheck, you're going to have to earn it. If you want a great relationship with your girlfriend, you're going to have to work at it.

DAY 208

PROVERBS 14:17–35

Again, if God is leading you to focus on one of the other verses that I can't get to here, then by all means, follow the Holy Spirit's lead! *Read today's passage.*

Verse 17 hits me right in the gut. I have acted foolishly when losing my temper, and nine out of every ten times when I hurt my wife's feelings, it's because I lost my temper and spoke foolishly. This is one of those things that is easy to understand intellectually, but *so ridiculously difficult* to implement when your temper flares. If you have problems keeping your temper in check, then give yourself a physical reminder, like a bracelet or mark on your hand that tells you to practice self-control, which is part of the fruit of the Spirit (Galatians 5:22–23).

Also, did you notice verse 24? I love it! "The foolishness of fools produces" what? It's not wealth; that's the wise. It's not friends; that's the wealthy (verse 20 and Proverbs 19:4). It's . . . wait for it . . . *more foolishness.*

Day 209

John 11:46-57

A renowned atheist recently made the big announcement that he had finally "developed" a philosophy of morality that he actually thought was separate from religious beliefs. His prime axiom? "Treat people the way you want them to treat you." This guy accidentally published a biblical teaching on his blog; he wanted so badly to get away from the Bible, but ended up arriving at the Bible's "golden rule." Oops! Similarly, as we close chapter 11, don't miss the part where one of the most corrupt and violent high priests Israel ever knew is used of God to accidentally prophesy the gospel (verses 50–52), though he meant something quite different. *Read today's Scripture.*

The Pharisees in your life can be used of Satan to drag you down, and they can speak words that they don't even realize are actually inspired by Satan (*especially* those who don't believe in Satan). However, they can also be the unwitting mouthpieces of God. Even the mob of hostile unbelievers is subject to the sovereignty of God, if not all the time, then at the ends of their lives. Let that bring you peace when you're persecuted. Let it also motivate you to evangelize.

JOHN 12:1–19

*R*ead today's text and see how you ought to eat: reclining like a boss! Mary, who in the last chapter was angry with Jesus, is now showing us how we ought to worship Him. She pours out her best at the feet of the King. This is also how we are to worship God with our finances. We are to pour out our best at the feet of the King. You are never too young to experience what a blessing it is to give back to the God who gave His life for you. Your money flows most quickly to that which is most important in your heart. Let it be toward the things of God.

Meanwhile, Jesus fulfills centuries-old prophecies in verses 12–16 without His disciples even realizing it until after the fact. And the Pharisees' plot to kill poor Lazarus (just imagine the events of these chapters from his perspective) proves futile as news of Jesus' raising Lazarus from the dead spreads. This just causes more to believe (verse 18). Don't listen to the Pharisees in your life. Don't listen to Judas. They are corrupt. Instead, just worship through giving as Mary does.

DAY 211

JOHN 12:20–36

As I write this at a coffee shop, there are two guys having a conversation that is obviously only meant for others to hear. *Awkward!* Though that example is on an infinitely smaller scale, it reminds me of what's going to happen in today's text when God the Father actually speaks to Jesus from heaven so that others would hear it (verse 28). *Read today's text.*

Jesus expressed His willingness to follow through with the coming crucifixion for the glory of God, and God spoke to prove it. The people didn't yet understand what was about to happen to Jesus, so Jesus encouraged them to believe in Him as the light because the darkness was coming. To drive this point home, He hid Himself after saying it. If you're on one of those youth-camp highs right now, then hold on to it, because the darkness is coming. If you're in the dark right now, then prove yourself to be a son of light (verse 36) by remembering who Jesus is despite His apparent absence right now.

Day 212

Proverbs 15:1–15

*R*ead today's Scripture. Verse 1 is your challenge for today: you will respond to someone who speaks harshly with a gentle answer. This is one of the most difficult things in the world for a man, but it is the sign of a strong man of godly character. It is also, go figure, the most effective way to deal with harsh people. Keep a level head and do not lose your cool.

Verse 9 is your reminder that God loves it when you pursue righteousness and strive to repent from sin. Go to great measures to practically secure repentance from lust and any other sins today, and know that God will love you for it.

Verse 15 is your goal. You will maintain the discipline of having a cheerful heart. In spite of trial, be cheerful. Also, be cheerful over things that you have taken for granted—things like the view out your window, the ability to run, and the way you love to play football and make music.

DAY 213

PROVERBS 15:16-17

If you have Jesus and nothing else, you have all that you need. If you lose all that you have, but hold on to your walk with Christ, you are a wealthy man and the envy of others. *Read today's text.*

This is such a sweet passage. Ambition is a good thing for a man to have. It is part of our construction as men to be providers, but do not fail to provide your future family with a leader who fears the Lord and who is full of love. I live and work in a very wealthy area, and many of the wealthy people I know who do not have God are some of the most miserable on the planet. They actually covet the peace that poorer Christians have because they can't buy it. Let your imagination develop the image of you at the dinner table with your future family today, and let that vision be one of a loving family that fears the Lord. Let your future family be wealthy in this way.

DAY 214

PROVERBS 15:18–33

*R*ead today's Scripture. Though, of course, all of these verses are amazing, verses 22 and 23 will be those you commit to memory today. Verse 22 has served me well personally many times. When big things show up in my life, I run them by my dad, my fellow pastors, and my brother. This approach has never let me down, and even non-Christians have found the same to be true outside the Bible. Challenge number 1 is to seek counsel today. However, be picky about your counselors. Choose only counselors whom you admire and want to be like.

Also, perhaps on the flip side of verse 22, you will be the one giving wise counsel so that someone else may succeed. Watch like a hawk and listen like a bat ("bat" as in Dracula, not Dustin Pedroia) for the chance to give an apt and wise reply just in time (verse 23)! So, today you will actively seek out your own verse 22 counsel while actively choosing to be someone else's verse 22 as you try to do verse 23.

DAY 215

JOHN 12:37–43

Even after seeing Jesus perform miracles with their own eyes, Jesus' detractors only hated Him even more and set into motion their plot to kill Him. *Read today's passage*.

Most of the people who saw these miracles had hard hearts like the hard soil Jesus talks about in the parable of the sower (Matthew 13). God hardened the hearts of the Pharisees because they still chose to be liked by their peers over siding with Jesus, even after Jesus proved beyond any reasonable doubt that He was the Messiah. Part of what makes following Jesus a step of faith is not only trusting in a God you cannot see, but also taking a risk that could cost you friendships. Don't betray your perfect God for your imperfect friends. Their eternity might be forever changed if you step out of line to do the unexpected thing: risk rejection for your faith. There is a chance that they might not hear you out because their hearts are hardened. There is also a chance that they would step from darkness into light. There is a chance they could be saved.

DAY 216

JOHN 12:44–50

In his book *Wild at Heart*, John Eldredge shows that every man needs a battle to fight, an adventure to live, and a beauty to rescue. Next to the book's outright invitation to be wild and dangerous like men are designed to be, the coolest thing about Eldredge's analysis is the parallel it draws between what every man needs and what God desires. They are the same, and we are integral to God's adventure. The church, often called the bride of Christ, is his beauty to rescue. Aspire to be like the ultimate example of masculinity. Aspire to be like Jesus: the One who rescues. *Read today's Scripture.*

I love verse 46. Jesus came to rescue us from darkness. He offers a perfect and heroic rescue for all who believe in Him. Be a man today and come to someone's rescue. As you do, let it be an act of worship. Let the act of rescuing someone in some way teach you more about who Jesus is.

DAY 217

JOHN 13:1–11

What you are about to read is the biggest scandal in history. Jesus washes His disciples' feet knowing that His disciple Judas has already been prompted (though not yet inhabited) by Satan to betray Him. The sight of Jesus wearing a towel around His waist was a huge shock to the disciples. In their society, Jesus should have been revered like a rabbi but was symbolically taking on the lowliest societal position possible, that of a servant with a towel ready. Also, the act of feet washing was utterly disgusting because people's feet were their primary mode of transportation. Shoes were open-toed, and toenail clipper technology wasn't quite what it is today. With that gross image in mind, *read today's Scripture*.

This scandalous act had nothing to do with foot hygiene. It was, according to verse 1, a demonstration of the full extent of Jesus' love. Jesus could have lassoed a star to demonstrate His love. He could have fashioned a fully-functioning PlayStation 5 out of mud for each of them. Instead, He washed their feet. It is one thing to love someone. It is *quite* another to foot-wash-love someone. Today, go foot-wash-love someone.

DAY 218

PROVERBS 16:1–9

I remember feeling the weight of major life decisions like college applications, a college major, a first job, and finding my wife. Whether or not these are the things on your mind right now, I know that this phase of life is fraught with intimidating decisions that determine your life's trajectory. That can be a lot of pressure, but *today's passage* could take a lot of weight off the bar.

God is sovereign. God is in charge. He allows man the freedom to mess up and make the wrong choice, but a man of God sets his heart on the things of God. As you face decisions today that will plot your ship's course, may you cast aside the maps you penned with a selfish heart and allow God to be your captain and navigator. According to verse 3, if we set sail for the shores where God's will waits, we will succeed.

DAY 219

PROVERBS 16:10–17

Brutal honesty. This is our focus today. *Read today's Scripture.*

So, clearly it is better to be forthright and honest, but this may require that you say the things that people don't want to hear or things that don't put you in the most positive light. The hardest part of being honest is being honest with yourself about your own performance and being honest with others about the results you produce. For men, it can often be hard to get real and speak honestly about where we stack up competitively. Speak the truth with brutal honesty even if you're being brutal to yourself. As verses 12 and 13 show, this will earn you tremendous respect. Be this man of brutal honesty and surround yourself with such men. Keep in mind, though, that being brutally honest does not require you to speak in a way that is uncharitable or rude. Rather, what makes a particular brand of honesty "brutal" is the uncompromising and unbiased content.

PROVERBS 16:18–25

The first verse you will read today is one that I could have recited from memory when I was blind to my own pride. Like controlling your temper and showing love to those who are not acting in a way that deserves a loving response, repentance from pride is one of those things that is easy to understand on an intellectual level but very difficult to live out. *Read today's Scripture.*

Memorize verse 18. Hide God's Word in your heart so that you may not sin against Him (Psalm 119:11). Hide God's Word in your hearts so that you won't suffer the destruction that follows pride. Depending on the circumstances, pride could bring about a fall because the prideful man's endeavors far overreach his capabilities out of his puffed-up view of himself. Remember yesterday's devotional? Yeah. Pride could also lead to a fall because, though a man is fully capable of achieving something, God sabotages his efforts in order to teach him humility the hard way. Did you understand that? I don't think you did. Read it again, because I wish I could go back in time and drill that truth into my prideful thick head when I was younger.

Day 221

Matthew 4:18–22

Let's get to know the author of 1 Peter. *Read today's Scripture.*

This takes place after the events of John 1. Finding Peter fishing at his age tells us that he was not a good student and was booted from Hebrew school. Only the absolute best students would get the chance to become disciples of a rabbi, and Jesus approaches this group of not-good-enoughs and gives them the rabbinic invitation to follow Him. This is why Peter and his bros drop their nets immediately to follow Jesus. Now, dropping their nets was a *huge* deal. Their nets were their livelihood and all they'd ever known.

My dad taught us how to cast-net fish when we were little. My cast net has my blood and saliva all over it. Part of throwing it involves putting the lead line that runs its circumference in my mouth (along with the occasional jellyfish). I know its weight and have thrown it so many times that you could drag me out of bed at 3:00 a.m. (please don't) and I could throw a decent circle with it. What is your net, and are you willing to drop it to follow Jesus? Drop your net today.

DAY 222

MATTHEW 14:22–31

This passage is simultaneously a triumph and a failure for Peter. *Read today's Scripture.*

Yes, Peter took his focus off of Jesus and put it on the storm and waves, and we can absolutely learn from that. But I'm still blown away by the fact that he walked on water for even one step at all. Get out of your boat today. In Jesus' name, I pray discomfort over you as you get out of your comfort zone and get out of your element just as Peter *literally* did.

For me, getting out of my boat is speaking about my son Aiden, who is in heaven. I simultaneously hate and love the fact that I'm called upon by fathers of sons who died at a young age. I hate the fact that I'm a part of that fraternity of grieving fathers, but I love the fact that my Aiden's story continues to impact people. Jesus is waiting for me on the rough waters, so I get out of my boat and speak. I'm not asking you to do something I don't. Get out of the boat and get uncomfortable.

DAY 223

MATTHEW 14:32-33

*R*ead today's passage. There is something fishy about the way Peter asked Jesus to call him in yesterday's verse 28. That's not really how a call works. If it were, I'd ask God to call me to be a rich pastor in Hawaii. I love how Jesus went with it, though. Peter fell into the water, and it became an epic teaching moment, but something bigger came out of it. Even though Peter "failed," it still had a huge impact on those watching from the boat.

Get out of the boat and go for it. Those with less faith are watching from the boat, and *even if you blow it,* people can still see that Jesus is Lord over the water and Lord over the storm. Even if you fall on your face, people can still come to see that Jesus is Lord. It is never a failure to share your faith. *It is a failure to never share your faith!*

DAY 224

JOHN 13:12–30

*R*ead today's Scripture. The other eleven disciples were completely fooled by Judas. He was stealing, but no one caught him; and even after Jesus' clear signal with the bread, they still didn't believe it. I think that we will be shocked who is and is not in heaven one day because Judases have a way of tricking the followers of Jesus.

Also, Jesus lays out this heavy command in verses 15 and 17, which gives us our challenge for the day. Jesus demonstrated the full extent of His love by washing His betrayer's feet and then told us to do the same. We are to wash one another's feet in a sense. I took this command literally on our wedding night and washed my wife's feet. Feel free to copy me on that one on your big day. You don't even have to give me credit for it: I stole the idea anyway. Back to Judas. Who is your Judas? Wash his feet through forgiveness today. Be like Jesus. I can tell you from experience that verse 17 is *absolutely* true. This insanely hard act of undeserved love does bring about an amazing reward. Wash your Judas's feet today.

JOHN 13:31–38

Chrome fish on the backs of cars, T-shirts that contort and spiritualize popular name brands, and cross necklaces are all ways to let your faith be known, but Jesus has a better way. *Read today's Scripture.*

Remember verses 36–38, because they will be important in our ongoing walk through Peter's life. Did you see how people will know we are Christians? It wasn't our old-school "W.W.J.D." bracelets, our Skillet albums blasting loudly, or even our Chick-fil-A addictions. It is our love. It is the love we have for our fellow Christians and our love for those who need Jesus. I like this type of proof better because a practicing pagan cannibal could buy a "McFaithald's: I'm lovin' it" T-shirt, but real love for people cannot be faked. Also, did you notice in verse 34 that this is a *command*? Whew, this command can be hard. Even when people are jerks, this command is still a command. It's not like Jesus built in some except-in-the-case-of-jerks clause. It is a command issued to us by our Savior without equivocation. Today, be a man of such great love that it is glaringly obvious that you are a Christian.

Day 226

John 14:1–4

My son Austin will go to great lengths to avoid being buckled into his seat. He uses karate, negotiation, and eventually resorts to just crying. The only thing that puts him at ease is when I tell him, "Son, don't be upset. I know you don't like this and don't understand it, but I'm *taking you home*." This is sort of like what Jesus tells His disciples in *today's text*.

Jesus always told people to back off when they wanted to crack down on His disciples' partying (Mark 2:18–20), and that's because He knew this time of suffering was coming. Like us today, they had many reasons to let their hearts be troubled, but Jesus says, "Trust in Me. I'm taking you home to the place I've prepared for you." Back then, when a man was engaged to a woman, he would build a room onto his father's house that would be the new home he shared with his bride. The church is the bride of Christ, and heaven is the awesome place that Christ has gone to prepare for His bride, the church. *And what an awesome place it is!* Check out Revelation 20. *He's taking you home!*

DAY 227

PROVERBS 16:26–33

I hope your heart is hungry. I hope you're an ambitious man. I hope that you're driven to succeed and to finish what you start. *Read today's Scripture.*

Let the wording of verse 26 paint a picture in your head. Envision this hardworking, hungry man. He is intensely motivated and singularly focused. He has a sense of direction and knows that he'll starve unless he achieves that to which he's called. I see a man squinting in the sunlight with sweat stinging his eyes. I see the left side of his tan upper lip curl as the burn of his empty stomach causes him to wince, and then I see him get back at it harder than ever. Be hungry, my student. Be a man who is hungry and be grateful for that appetite because, according to verse 26, that is what drives you to succeed.

Also, in light of verse 31, go easy on your old man for his gray hair.

Day 228

Proverbs 17:1–5

Read today's passage. Hold verse 1 in one hand and hold your future plans for your career and family in the other. Weigh them. Are they balanced? I have worked with thousands of teenagers, and many of them would much rather their fathers earn *less* money in exchange for *more* time with the family. If it's God's will that you become a family man one day, then know now that you will stand in judgment not primarily for how fast you climbed the corporate ladder, but how you treated the precious wife and children God gave you.

Verse 2 shows the benefits of being able to deal with spoiled brats. This servant was so good with the little brat that he actually shared in the kid's inheritance! Verse 5 reveals much about God's heart. He is fiercely protective over the poor and afflicted to the point that He will punish those who mock them. Today's reading offers you a Now and Later challenge. Have a banana-flavored chewy while you consider how this passage wants you to treat others, both now and in the future.

Day 229

Proverbs 17:6–8

Trying to seem intelligent by using words you don't actually understand is kind of like a hungry velociraptor trying to blend in at a preschool. Picture that right now. It doesn't work, and we're all completely onto your obvious plot. (Though it's unlikely that your species is extinct and that you would eat a child.) *Read today's Scripture.*

Big words are appropriate for academic settings, scholarly discussions, and teaching environments, where they can be defined. Outside of those settings, though, they can backfire big-time on the guy who uses them to appear intelligent. If big words just roll out of your mouth naturally and that's just who you are, then rock on, but make sure you speak in a way that's understood. Think about how ironically dumb it is for an intelligent person to speak in a way that people don't get. If you aren't 100 percent certain about what you're saying, then *don't say it.* That's the point that verse 7 makes: *speak truthfully.* Part of speaking truthfully is knowing what you're saying and saying it without pretense.

DAY 230

MATTHEW 16:13–20

Today, Simon Peter's name officially becomes Peter as Jesus prophesies what Peter's purpose will be in life. *Read today's Scripture.*

This really brings us back to the concept of identity, but in two applications this time. First, Peter was *named* for his purpose. Jesus said, "You are Peter, and on this rock I will build my church." His identity was built upon God's purpose for him, just as yours should be. Let God's purpose for your life be just as integral to your identity as your name. Let the two be spoken together always. "Yeah, that's Peter, and he's the guy God used to launch the church as we know it." "Yeah, that's Chris, and he's the only Christian on the football team but isn't the least bit shy about it." The other application regarding identity that flows from this text is the way you identify Jesus. Who is Jesus to you? Is He a historical figure, a miracle worker, or is He your Lord? Your answer has direct bearing on your identity.

Speaking of Peter saying that Jesus was the Christ, have the Andrew and Philip in your life made a spiritual impact of their own? Pray for your Andrew, Philip, and Peter.

DAY 231

MATTHEW 16:21–23

Peter is about to get verbally slammed in the worst way possible. This is the second lowest point in Peter's walk with the physical Jesus. *Read today's Scripture.*

Peter's walk with Jesus has been such a roller coaster, hasn't it? Earlier in this same chapter, he was blessed by Jesus. Why did Jesus call him Satan? Peter had just pulled his rabbi and Savior aside to correct Him for one thing, but also Peter was denying that Jesus would do what Jesus was born to do: save believers from their sins. Peter's "correction" bears an eerie similarity to Satan's temptation in Matthew 4:8–9 when he offered Jesus dominion without the cross. Peter had not fully counted the cost of following Jesus. Sure, he dropped his net, but he wasn't ready for the dark and heavy death stuff. Peter wasn't ready to see Jesus suffer, but some things only come about by suffering. Do you want the easy, G-rated Christian life? Peter did in this passage, and Jesus called him "Satan." Be honest with God about the degree to which you are willing to suffer for the gospel. Be willing to follow Jesus even to the cross.

DAY 232

MATTHEW 16:24–26

Read today's passage. Lose your life today. Lose your plans and dreams to the plans and dreams that God has for you. If you forsake the plans and calling that God has for you so that you can pursue your own thing instead, you may waste your life and enter eternity empty-handed. If you forsake your plans in exchange for God's will, you take hold of the life that is truly life (1 Timothy 6:18–19). This is the meaning of verse 25.

Verse 26 drives this point home further by showing how futile it is for a man to achieve all of his wildest dreams and take over the world, but forfeit his soul by not following Jesus. By the way, this does not mean that you can never see your own desires fulfilled or experience your own brand of success in any way. Rather, it shows how much greater heavenly success is than earthly success. The longest life lived on the earth does not yield a measurable fraction of the time spent in eternity. So, deny yourself, take up your cross (a tool for brutal execution), and follow Jesus. Being a disciple of Christ could cost you everything.

DAY 233

JOHN 14:5–6

As a Christian man, you will face accusations of arrogance. *Ready today's Scripture.*

Love people enough to stand by verse 6. *Do not ever back down* from this. Backing down and letting a nonbeliever hear a Christian even suggest by way of surrender that there is another way to be saved besides Jesus is practically sealing that nonbeliever's fate to hell. Christianity does not play well with other religions because Christianity is truth and that is the nature of truth. We agree that 2+2=4, right? And I hope that you are close-minded about that, because to be open to the idea that 2+2= squirrels is foolish. Similarly, Jesus says that *no one* goes to heaven except through Him, and it is foolish verging on hateful to let people think they are going to heaven without Jesus. If they shoot you down, then stick to your guns, but at least don't let the non-Christians in your life be shocked on judgment day. More importantly, if they shoot you down, they are actually shooting Jesus down here because it was Jesus who first said these words. If people object to these words, then they will have to take that up with Jesus, not you.

DAY 234

JOHN 14:7–14

The man of God puts down his plans for his life and picks up God's. But when that man does so, he taps into a strength that is far beyond the sum of his skills, experiences, and aspirations. A man who channels the power of God can endure and achieve anything. He whose prayer life is a constant stream of communication evoking (calling upon) the name of Jesus will go on to see greater miracles than Jesus' healings! Sounds crazy? *Read today's Scripture.*

I believe that a sinner being saved is the greatest miracle there is, and we as evangelists get to speak to other sinners on Jesus' behalf now that He has gone to the Father. We get a front row seat to the greatest of miracles. Because Jesus and the Father are one and because Jesus invites us to drop His name in prayer to the Father, we have the Father's power at our disposal to carry out whatever aligns with the Father's will. A selfish and futile prayer (remember James 4:3?) in Jesus' name uses the Lord's name in vain (Exodus 20:7), but a sinner praying in repentance will always be answered, "*Yes!*"

DAY 235

JOHN 14:15–31

I don't just tell my wife that I love her. I prove it by doing dishes, changing diapers, and completing the "honey-do" list. Similarly, our love for Jesus will be proven by our obedience to His commands. *Read today's text.*

Immediately after this teaching about obedience is the foretelling of the Holy Spirit's coming and a groundbreaking teaching about the Trinity. When you feel conviction for sin, God's presence during worship, and a compulsion to do the will of God along with the people of God, that is brought about by the Holy Spirit. Jesus was the direct presence of God on the earth; today that presence is the Holy Spirit. The result is this incredible and inexplicable peace (Philippians 4:7).

I have sat in a waiting room while my son's body was open on an operating table and felt this peace. May you abide in and live by (Romans 8) the Holy Spirit today and be filled with peace. May you listen to this Holy Spirit's conviction as it draws you away from pride, pornography, and all sin. I know it sounds kind of hippieish and weird, but this is grown-man Christianity.

DAY 236

PROVERBS 17:8

Bribes, unfortunately, are effective, and their success depends upon the fallibility (the flawed nature) of man's character and on man's love of money over integrity. To bribe someone is basically to pay him money to do something unethical for you or just to keep him under your control, and people do it quite a bit. Now, before you picture some old-school mob boss with a fedora and a luxury car with tinted windows, know that a practice like bribery is carried out by loving parents and grandparents every day. Of course, it's perfectly legal, but this form of "bribery" is carried out when a man who is perfectly capable of paying his own way and even has a family of his own takes orders from those who help him pay his bills. *Ready today's verse.*

For one thing, it's important that you're not naive. The true point of this proverb is that people will get what they want through crooked ways, but you as a man of God who lives by the Holy Spirit are expected to stay squeaky-clean. People around you are going to bribe. They are going to cheat. Get over it and keep your integrity. The other application of this idea, however, is not to let yourself be controlled by money. My dad always told me, "Jess, be your own man."

DAY 237

PROVERBS 17:9

Read today's verse. Most fights that break out among men are meaningless fights. They come about because a man lacks wisdom and patience (Proverbs 19:11). What the world considers reason to throw down on a guy usually doesn't fly with God. You *will* be offended. You *will* be let down. Does that shock you? For that matter, *you* will offend people, and *you* will let people down from time to time. It takes a strong, strong man of God to forego his "right" to be offended and instead promote love.

There is a good chance you'll be offended today, but when you are, you are going to overlook it if it does no harm to anyone or anything other than your ego. Take a deep breath, swallow hard, and read Proverbs 17:9.

PROVERBS 17:10

Read today's verse. To a man of wisdom, being rebuked is a big deal. Also, did you notice what a tough hide this fool must have? One hundred lashes. I mean . . . seriously? He didn't get the message on whipping number two, three, or fifty? Did it cross his mind in the neighborhood of lash number eighty-nine that, "Maybe I should change course here"? It's far better to learn a lesson from a rebuke than from some harder form of retribution. Right now, at your current phase of life, the stakes are probably lower than they will ever be. One day, you'll have a house and an established career on the line. Don't be the fool in this passage, who has to take multiple punishments before he learns his lesson. Instead, be the wise man and take your lesson from the warning.

DAY 239

MATTHEW 26:69–75
(Back to Peter's story . . .)

At the end of the Last Supper, Peter made the bold proclamation that he would lay down his life to follow Jesus, and Jesus called him out, prophesying that Peter would deny that he even knew Jesus three times before the rooster crowed that night. *Read today's text.* We'll see another perspective on this story as we finish the gospel of John.

Peter's grandiose promises just fell to pieces. In a single night, he went from cutting a man's ear off to cowering at the accusations of a servant girl. Even though the accusation of verse 73 was based on his accent, I still hope that accusation could be leveled against you; I hope people can tell you are a follower of Jesus based on the way that you speak. In verse 75, it all comes crashing down on Peter, and he realizes that his bold proclamations were just hot air. Before you get too hard on Peter, though, take an inventory of any big promises you've made to your group at church at your last big event when you were spiritually high as a kite. Have you followed through with your proclamations?

DAY 240

JOHN 21:1–19

(Peeking ahead in the gospel of John for Peter's story)

So, after Peter abandoned and publicly denied Jesus three times at the time of Jesus' greatest vulnerability, one might think that visiting Peter would have been pretty low on the resurrected Jesus' to-do list. Yet Peter was one of the *first* people to see the resurrected Jesus. Think for a minute on what that reveals about the nature of God. *Read today's passage.*

What a beautiful redemption for Peter. It was painful (verse 17), but perfect. Now, understand that Peter wasn't making atonement for abandoning Jesus. Jesus had already atoned for sin on the cross. Instead with these three restorative questions (one for each of Peter's denials), Jesus was bringing healing to Peter's aching heart. There Peter was doing exactly what he was doing when he was first called; he was fishing. Have you ever gone back to the things you did before you were saved? You can't go back; things are never the same. You can't pretend that you never knew Jesus. However, even when we publicly deny Jesus, He still makes breakfast on the beach. He still loves and restores us. Come home today.

DAY 241

ACTS 2:14–41

Because so many of her friends invited her persistently, a young woman who was a publicly avowed atheist at her school started coming to our church's student ministry. After months of objectively weighing Christianity, she took a step of faith and was saved. She told me she best related to Peter, who, like her, had taken a public vow that she would never know Christ and become a Christian. Today, she is still paralleling Peter's story in some ways. She is in ministry proclaiming the gospel to the lost just like Peter does in *today's Scripture*.

Today, you are going to do what Peter did in verse 14. Wow! Talk about radical transformation—to go from cowering at a little girl's accusations to loudly, directly, and even confrontationally speaking the gospel to a crowd. God used someone who had disowned him to lead about three thousand people to Christ (verse 41). Just imagine what God can do through you!

DAY 242

JOHN 15:1–8

The setting was tense. Jesus seemed to be teaching at a rapid-fire pace that night, and Judas hadn't been seen since dinner. Though they were pretty confused, the disciples soon began to see that this would be their last lesson with Jesus. Jesus picked up a grapevine that may have grown for this very purpose and began to talk about, of all things, pruning, which is the process of cutting away the parts of a plant that don't bear fruit or are dying. *Read today's Scripture.*

This teaching is twofold. First, those Christians who don't bear fruit (good works done in Jesus' name, people led to or at least impacted for Christ, etc.) were apparently not Christians to begin with (Matthew 7:21). Second, those Christians who do bear fruit will be "pruned" so that they can bear much fruit. Pruning can be painful, as not only sinful habits, but basically good things that distract you from bearing much fruit are cut away (Hebrews 12:1). Are you being pruned right now? Invite and be grateful for this cutting away of lesser things so that all of your time, gifts, and energy can be focused on that which bears *much* fruit for God's kingdom.

DAY 243

JOHN 15:9–17

Jesus builds upon what He laid out yesterday and arrives at a message that may have inspired Peter's instructions to the church in Rome in the year 64 under Nero's persecution. *Read today's Scripture.*

It makes sense. Peter learned how to coach that church based on the persecution he and his fellow disciples would experience. In 1 Peter 4, he was basically just passing Jesus' teaching on from John 15. He knew that a fierce love among believers was necessary because Jesus taught him that it was. Also, let it blow your mind that Jesus would call you a friend (verses 13–14). Because you have been so commanded and because it is the ultimate act of masculinity and friendship, practice self-sacrifice today and show love to your fellow Christians in a deliberate way. That means get out your phone and send a mass text or online message. That means bring some doughnuts to Bible study. That means go cut some grass for people.

Speaking of loving people, how are Andrew and Philip? Have they come to know Christ and begun to bear fruit of their own?

DAY 244

JOHN 15:18–27

There are some people out there who hate me. If you were to put a picture of me up on some street corners, there would be more than one hole in it by the day's end. A couple of people I knew years ago expressed their hatred for me because (oddly) I refused to drink alcohol when I was underage. A few more hate me because I stand by the Bible's teachings in Romans 1, and the others, I don't know, though I bet it has something to do with Jesus. *Read today's text*.

Today, keep three things in mind:

1. There are Christians around the world in countries like North Korea, Iran, and Sudan who are being persecuted for their beliefs to the point of facing death, so buck up.
2. Some people will hate Jesus through you.
3. If you don't catch even a little bit of heat for your faith, then you're not living it loudly enough. Take resistance from the enemy as a sure sign that you remind him of Jesus!

Day 245

Proverbs 17:11–16

Again, be sure to follow the Holy Spirit's lead to focus on whatever verse or verses convict you the most, though we can only focus on a couple for this devotional entry. *Read today's passage.*

First off I love the mental picture that verse 12 paints. According to that verse, if you are forced to join either your buddy in his ironically named "foolproof" plan to knock over an ATM or face a momma bear who has been robbed of her cubs, you should go with the man-eating grizzly every time. Remember that if you're ever on a game show. You can cite this verse and say, "Argue with God, Trebek. I'm right!"

Now, get a pen and write out verse 14 on your hand. It may come in *handy* today. *Bahahaha! . . . Sigh . . .*

DAY 246

PROVERBS 17:17–20

It may be a misapplication of the verse, but I think about how verse 17 describes my son Aiden being born without a trachea and the beneficial role his twin brother, Asher, had in being near him through his life. *Read today's text.*

My family's difficult time brought us closer to our families, and it forged new friendships with those who walked through the fire with us. Be grateful for those friends in your life now. Think about those who have stuck by your side through the highs and the lows, and strive to be that kind of friend today.

Also, you can use verse 18 to tell your broke friend, "No, bro," when he asks you to cosign on the loan for his overpriced sports car.

DAY 247

PROVERBS 17:21–26

Read today's Scripture. You have to fight like an electrocuted rabid bobcat for your joy sometimes. (Picture it . . . *piiictuuurre it* . . . no, not that . . . *there* it is. *Ha!*) It's just good medicine to have a joyful heart. Satan will try to give you a thousand reasons not to have a joyful heart while also trying to subtract from the reasons you *do* have. A broken spirit can, as verse 22 says, dry you up from the very core of your structure, your bones. Satan knows this, and he knows that it fits his purposes best to rob Christians of their joy. So put up a fight today. Your joy may not be everything, but it is so important, and it flows from the Holy Spirit living within you (Galatians 5 again).

Also, did you catch verses 21 and 25? Please, be a good son to your father while you're at it.

DAY 248

EPHESIANS 5:3-4

How far is too far when it comes to compromising your purity? How much can you get away with before it's sin? *Read today's text!*

Boom. There shouldn't be *even a hint* of sexual immorality in your life. It shouldn't "even be heard of"! So, does the quasi-sexually-inappropriate action X count as sin? Well, if the quasi-sexually-inappropriate action X hints at, sounds like, resembles, or even rhymes with sexual immorality, then *yes*. So, repent. Be ruthless with your sexual sin. Go to drastic measures to be a man of holiness. Throw your computer into the path of an approaching ice-cream truck before you let yourself drown in a pornography addiction. Cut the relationship off (if just for a time) before you do any more damage to your purity, and if you do get back together, never find yourselves alone again. "Jesse, you're being too drastic." No! I'm telling you what it realistically takes to live by Ephesians 5:3-4. God has high standards for you, man of God. Go do whatever it takes immediately. Draw a line in the sand and pick a fight with your sin. Choose God.

Why are you still reading?! *Go!*

DAY 249

JOHN 16:1–15

A torrent of persecution was about to fall on the disciples, and the people doing the persecuting would not be pagans, per se, but religious leaders in the worship of Yahweh! In fact, the people who executed the disciples did so thinking that they were actually honoring God as they did. The disciples were not alone in this fight, though. They had the Holy Spirit. *Read today's Scripture.*

This was heavy and troubling news to the disciples, but Jesus knew they needed to hear it (verses 6–7). It's also a vivid description of the Holy Spirit's purpose in the world: to convict the world of sin because it doesn't believe in Jesus, for righteousness with integrity because Jesus would soon disappear to go to the Father, and for judgment because the world judged Jesus while Jesus was the Judge of the world.

Some of the worst grief you'll experience in your Christian life will be brought on not just by militant atheists, but by religious people who lack or do not live by the Holy Spirit.

DAY 250

JOHN 16:16–28

*R*ead *today's Scripture.* In verse 20, Jesus confirms the fears and validates the sorrow of the disciples as He shocks and grieves them with this final teaching. Moreover, He assures them that the world will rejoice over their hardship. Nice, huh? No, not nice . . . *good.* There is a difference. Jesus was giving His disciples the harsh truth.

And I'm thankful, *eternally* thankful, that He also has equally effective words of comfort and hope. Verse 22 applies to you and me today as we await God's return or our own trips to heaven: "So you also have sorrow now. But I will see you again. Your hearts will rejoice, and no one will rob you of your joy." See that? Jesus knows that we will have sorrow now. You can no longer think that having sorrow means God's not around. Jesus warned you about it here! Instead, clutch this verse and know that your sorrow will be crushed by the joy you will experience in Jesus' direct presence one awe-filled day.

DAY 251

JOHN 16:29–33

Even a blind squirrel finds a nut every now and then. Today, as Jesus speaks His last message before the crucifixion, the disciples finally begin to get it. *Liiiiight bulb! Read today's text.*

When people asked me how I could keep my faith through all the suffering of losing a son, the question crossed me as obscure. God never told us that bad things wouldn't happen to us. He never said it would be easy. He said in verse 33 that we *will have suffering* in this world, but to be courageous and take heart because Jesus has conquered this world! Heaven is that coming time when we will no longer know suffering or evil or death or pain. Anyone who expects this life to be heaven is ignorant of the Bible and in for a shock. In verse 33, Jesus clarifies that He tells us these things so that we may have peace through Him. So, today, walk in that peace knowing that Jesus has already overcome the things that bring us suffering in this life and that we will be with Him soon to share as coheirs in that victory. Say aloud to your suffering, "Jesus has overcome you."

DAY 252

PROVERBS 17:27–28

We studied the value of silence way back in the book of James, but if you're anything like me, I'll bet it's time for a refresher. *Read today's verses.*

Once you've lost your cool and said the wrong thing, you can't un-say it. Don't be trigger-happy with your words; be selective. You are the picky judge with bad hair on the talent reality show, and your words are the hopeful ones auditioning to be spoken. This is especially important in the world of social media because a public record is kept of your careless words if you blow it online.

The funny thing about verse 28 is that it's not only wise advice for the wise, but an observation about the foolish. I've been impressed with people in the past . . . until they spoke. *Ha!*

Now, that's a useful trick. The value of silence indeed.

DAY 253

PROVERBS 18:1

Men need to walk alongside other men. *Read today's verse*. The Christian life is hard enough with accountability, but it's downright impossible to walk all by yourself. When you're a lone wolf, you only go after your own goals and are robbed of the chance to fight alongside another. This is not only sort of dangerous but also unbiblical. It is downright contradictory to Philippians 2:4, which says, "Everyone should look out not only for his own interests, but also for the interests of others." The second half of this verse speaks to the way a lone wolf will rebel against all sound judgment because he has no other man of God to share wise counsel with him and call him out when he is acting in a way that is out of line with godly convictions.

Did you ever follow up with those godly, wise friendships we wanted to cultivate back when we studied Proverbs 13:20? Before you get up from wherever it is you're sitting right now, make an effort if possible to connect yourself spiritually with other men. You need them.

DAY 254

PROVERBS 18:2

Read today's verse. Do you know someone like that? Think about it. If no one comes to mind, then you know what that means. Yep, it could be *you*! When someone speaks to you, do you just think about what you're going to say when he finally stops yapping, instead of actually listening to what he's saying? When a discussion comes up about which you have an opinion (or just desperately want to be a part of), do you feel this anxiety swelling up from within you and fighting to get out so that people will know your opinion, even though it's not necessary? I've been there, and I still feel that way sometimes.

It's often way better to be asked for your input. That way, you earn people's respect when they hear that you have had a germane and educated opinion all along, but have been hearing everyone else out first. Absolutely, speak up when it's important enough, but know that people get tired of the guy who throws in his opinion every single time. Strive to be respected when you speak. This way, when it's time to bring up the gospel, you will be heard.

DAY 255

JOHN 17:1–19

We are incredibly privileged today. We are about to listen in on the final extended prayer that Jesus prayed in His earthly body. His cruci-fiers are closing in. A militia led by His betrayer will arrive any moment. What does the Son of God pray? Let's listen in as we *read today's text*.

After praying for Himself—that He would be brought back to the glory in which He existed before the world was made . . . *whoa*—He prays for His disciples. The main theme of His prayer for them is pro-tection (verses 12–15). He prayed that they would be in harm's way. Jesus never intended for you just to stay at home, wrapped in bubble wrap, wearing your helmet, lying in your bomb shelter. He prayed for His disciples to be protected as they are about to be isolated in a world that hates them.

Get out of the Christian bubble. Get out of your own insulated world and look to the rough world around you, full of people who des-perately need Jesus. Get in harm's way knowing that God will protect you. Be a man. You've been commissioned, remember?

Day 256

John 17:20–26

Yesterday's prayer was for the disciples specifically, but today's is more directly prayed for you and me because we are those who believe in Jesus through the disciples' message. For crying out loud, we're reading the gospel of *John*—one of Jesus' disciples! This prayer is for *you. Read today's Scripture.*

The theme of Jesus' prayer for us is one of unity (verses 21–22 especially). The thrust of Jesus' prayer for His disciples *applies* to you and me, but this was prayed *for* you and me. My dad used to pray over our meals, "We thank You, Father, for the unity and bond of love that we share." I never knew until I really studied this passage that the unity for which my father thanked my Father was a fulfillment of the prayer of the Son in John 17:20–26. You need unity with other believers. You need unity with fellow men. It is so important that it was the very last thing Jesus prayed for before the crucifixion began.

Day 257

John 18:1–3

Based on what we learned of Jesus' emotional response to Lazarus's death, we know that He still felt pain over the things He even foreknew would happen. It was prophesied all the way back in Psalms, which is centuries older than the Gospel of John, that the Messiah would be betrayed by someone close to him, someone with whom He shared bread (Psalm 41:9). Bread sharing was a big deal. So, apply that Christological (the study of Christ) truth to *today's passage*.

Ugh . . . Verse 2 just makes my heart hurt for Christ. Judas led these armed men to a place where he and Jesus shared memories. It was a garden where Jesus would go to retreat and pray. It was a personal place, and Judas brought the enemy into it. For that matter, he didn't just bring the enemy to it; he was inhabited by the enemy, and the enemy brought men with lanterns, torches, and *weapons*! These men were obviously satanically hostile and/or completely deceived. Jesus never hurt, but only healed. That you might know Him better, speak to God in prayer about the wound dealt to His heart by this terrible betrayal. You see, He knows what it's like.

DAY 258

PROVERBS 18:3-21

This is crazy: I didn't plan for the first verse of today's devotional to align so perfectly with the last verse of yesterday's, but they do. Seriously, what are the odds of this? It must be God hammering this point home to us. It is more likely sovereignty (God making it happen) than coincidence (chance). *Read today's Scripture.*

Today, we consider the power of our words. They are a matter of life and death (verse 21). They can lead to strife, beatings, and devastation (verses 6–7); taste like delicious, poisonous foods (verse 8); and offend a brother to the point that he's impossible to reach (verse 19). Much of the course of your life is determined by your words (verse 20). Speak with your future in mind today.

Day 259

Proverbs 18:22–24

Read today's verses. Aw, yeah! Verse 22 just happened! I love how practical it is. I love how . . . almost mathematical it is. I'm sorry to the touchy-feely Christians who think your wife is brought to your lazy tail as you sit there in your sweat lodge alone with your feelings. *Ha!*

This verse butts up against the idea of a soul mate pretty hard. Here's how it works according to Proverbs 18:22: you find a wife, and you please the Lord. I know *so* many men my age who have been waiting around for some woman so perfect she's like the female version of Jesus. They have been waiting, *waiting* on their perfect 11s. Meanwhile, bro is like a 6, if he's honest. Now, does God sovereignly set you up to be able to make this move? Absolutely (Proverbs 19:14). When the time comes in your life to go out and get your Proverbs 31 woman, I hope you're a Proverbs 18 man, and when someone starts pitching the soul-mate philosophy, you compare everything he says to Proverbs 18:22. Many of the guys who don't get this are single and will be single until they get it.

DAY 260

PROVERBS 19:1–14

Continuing with this theme of thinking about your future wife and marriage, *read today's Scripture.*

Do you know of a Proverbs 19:13b marriage? It's when a wife refuses to submit to her husband's leadership (Ephesians 5:22), and instead of just following his lead and trusting God, she tries to be his mother and nags him until he changes. There comes a time when a nagging wife gets her way, and the husband just decides he doesn't love her enough to resist anymore. He caves. Like a tamed stallion, he goes where he is told at all times and never runs again. So, the nagging Proverbs 19:13b woman should be happy, right? She is victorious and has gotten her way, right? No, she is alone in the world without her protector and fellow parent. Keep this in mind as you scan the horizon for your future wife, but keep in mind that any woman can go through a phase like this that ends in repentance.

God, however, can bring you a sensible wife, a reasonable, patient, and gracious wife. Think about her. Hear her voice. In Jesus' name, may your future wife be such a woman.

HEBREWS 12:14–17 AND
GENESIS 25:29–34

Committing sexual sin is selling yourself short and robbing yourself of what God has in store for you. *Read Hebrews 12:14–17.* The Greek word for "immorality" in this verse is *pornos* of the root word *pornea* from which we get *pornography*, and it is often translated as *immorality*, but can also refer to *sexual immorality* depending on its context. Now, *read Genesis 25:29–34.*

Esau gave away a massive monetary inheritance and his title as the next patriarch of Israel. Granted, God proclaimed that He would oppose Esau before the twins were born, and Jacob was a conniving little trickster in the way he stole the birthright, but the foolishness of Esau's decision here is still shocking. It was very much like the sin of adultery and lust in general. Through marriage and its capacity for the most amazing sex life possible, God has set you up with an inheritance, and compromising that for immediate and temporary gratification is much like giving up your birthright for a bowl of lentil soup. I seriously just had some lentils today. They weren't all that good. Don't sell yourself short and live with regret like Esau. Instead, hold out for the great inheritance.

DAY 262

JOHN 18:4–11

Jesus was the ultimate presence: God's power manifest in masculine form. He was absolute power incarnate but was gentle. It was rare for Him to be aggressive at all, but He is about to be confronted by Judas's angry mob. *Read today's Scripture.*

What incredible power. Just the statement that He is who He is literally knocked this crowd to the ground! That He would use the words "I am" harked back to the way Yahweh introduced Himself to Moses through the burning bush before Israel even existed as a nation. Also, there goes Peter in verses 10 and 11. Jesus, according to other Gospel perspectives, does heal this poor guy's ear, by the way. Peter is practically up to his old tricks for which Jesus referred to him as "Satan" because Peter *still* acted as though he could prevent from happening exactly that which all of mankind needed to happen.

Jesus knows His name in this text and beyond (Revelation 19:12) and speaks it with such overwhelming presence that His enemies are knocked over by this "introduction." As you imitate the ultimate masculine, be who you are, and let others respond as they might. You know your name.

DAY 263

JOHN 18:12–27

If you and three of your buddies were caught rolling a house and brought in for questioning (which wouldn't happen, by the way), the four of you would together describe your own perspectives of the rolling. Some of you would have more insight into aspects of the night than others, but this doesn't mean that you guys are lying. It just means that you have different perspectives. The four Gospel writers may have shared Mark's notes (synoptic theory) and been inspired by the Holy Spirit from there to provide their own perspectives. *Read today's passage.*

John's perspective reveals some inside connections we didn't realize existed from our previous tours of other Gospel perspectives. For example, Annas (verses 13–14) is father-in-law to the high-priest turned accidental-prophet Caiaphas. Also, the girl who lets him in at the order of Caiaphas, who knew one of the disciples, is the same doorkeeper whose accusations bring Peter to his knees spiritually. Next, Peter warms himself next to one of the high priest's slaves, who is related to . . . wait for it . . . the dude whose ear Peter just chopped off!

Peter was trying to get cozy next to his own persecutors. Like you, he should've known he wouldn't blend in.

DAY 264

JOHN 18:28-40

Be prepared. You live in a culture and age in which the nature of truth itself has eroded. It's ironic that views of truth like ours (absolute-truth views) are absolutely considered wrong. To absolutely condemn any absolute view is to have an absolute view! Many non-Christians who claim to be open-minded are ironically very close-minded when it comes to Christianity. *Read today's passage.*

Pilate's question in verse 38 is that of our age. Here is your answer: truth is like math, and you are either right or wrong. Jesus is the truth (John 14:6), and you're either saved or not. What was especially maddening about this was the way the crowd wanted a convicted murderer to be released instead of Jesus (verse 40). Go figure. Their leader doesn't know what truth is, and they as a crowd immediately release a dangerous felon. Raise your hand if you're shocked.

Now, what brings me comfort is the fact that God is still in charge even though the crazy, confused people have the titles. God used them to bring about the fulfillment of His prophecies in verse 32 and still does this today with equally confused people.

Day 265

Proverbs 19:15–21

Read today's Scripture. This small collection of proverbs covers a lot of ground, and verse 17 is not to be overlooked. Let's start with today's challenge: I want you to show kindness to a poor person today. I spoke with another author who once lived the homeless lifestyle for three months in three major cities, and he shared with me the best way to bless a needy person: go pick up some five-dollar gift cards from a fast-food restaurant and give them away to people who need them. Verse 17 says that you will be rewarded, but your motivation is in love and not that reward. Let it be said with good reason that you are a generous man.

Speaking of the kind of man you are, let's think about the end game again. Let's think about the long haul. Fix your eyes to the horizon of your life right now and let verses 20 and 21 set you on an upward trajectory. Now is the time to begin becoming a wise older man, and the beginning of wisdom is fear of the Lord. Know that God is ultimately in charge (verse 21). Be generous today. Be wise tomorrow.

DAY 266

PROVERBS 19:22-29

I have given my life to ministry and have learned that the most valuable traits are not necessarily speaking ability, administrative skill (because I have *none*), or good looks (of which I have *plenty* . . . *ha!*), but integrity and trustworthiness. It is so incredibly important to follow through with what you start. If I announce to my students that some event will happen and then don't follow through with it, then their trust for me erodes. If I speak like Winston Churchill (Google him), but I'm really just a fake, then I'm worthless as a minister. Integrity and trustworthiness are of utmost importance. *Read today's Scripture.*

Wow, did you catch verse 22? (Ah! Get it? "Catch 22"? No? . . . Okay, moving on.) It's better to be an honest poor man than a rich liar. Integrity and trustworthiness are the most desirable things in a man, and that's not just true in the context of ministry and the professional world. It's true in masculine fellowship, and it is *massively* true in romantic relationships. Just as a church would rather have an upright pastor who speaks poorly than a smooth-talking cheater, a woman would rather be married to a homely honest man than a handsome liar.

Day 267

Proverbs 20:1–4

Let's talk about alcohol. I'll make this really easy for you: it's illegal to drink underage. Done. That's your reason if you ever find yourself in the dangerous situation wherein you're surrounded by underage drinkers at a party or something. I was amazed when a former student of mine asked me what he should say to the guys who were pressuring him to drink before he was old enough. "You tell them *no*, genius!" was my reply. If they ask you why, then you can use the reason that you are underage until you are of age, at which point you need to know what the Bible says about alcohol. *Read today's Scripture.*

The Bible does not condemn drinking as a sin. In fact, wine was a prominent element in Jesus' miracles and teachings. However, the Bible is *crystal* clear about getting drunk, and Paul writes in Romans 14 that we should consider others when it comes to our convictions on the matter. Remember, you are a man after *wisdom,* and verse 1 clearly says that the man who gets drunk and staggers (HCSB) is not wise. Read this next sentence twice: Choose God's wisdom over your friends' acceptance.

Acts 15:36–41

At times, you won't be liked. You'll have disputes. You'll have confrontations. These are a part of being men, and even the godliest Christian men will not see eye-to-eye all the time. Conflict is unavoidable for the man who truly stands for something. In fact, you could say that the absence of conflict and being winsome (likeable) to the point that *everyone* likes you is an indicator that you don't stand for anything. *Read today's text.*

Conflict in itself is not a bad thing, and some good things can only come from healthy conflict. Here are Paul and Barnabas, two of the most amazing men of God to have lived, in a conflict so sharp that it leads to the two of them parting ways. Don't forsake who you are or your convictions so that someone will like you. If you are disliked by someone and don't know why, then let *that person* deal with who you are. If you need to part ways, then do so without sweating it. If you need to deal with conflict, then do it in accordance with Jesus' instructions in Matthew 18:15–20 by starting man-to-man.

DAY 269

JOHN 19:1–7

There's this old-school movie that is a funny version of the Arthurian legend. In one scene, King Arthur "rides" up to a peasant woman and tells her that he is her king. She responds, "I didn't know we had a king" (*Monty Python and the Holy Grail*). I think of that woman often. When it comes to King Jesus, some might think, *I didn't know we lived in a monarchy.* Whether we acknowledge it or not, Jesus is King! *Read today's Scripture.*

Remember Pilate and his slick ways. For now, however, notice how these people *mocked* Jesus' proclaimed kingship. That's unwise. If I were pulled over for speeding and told the officer that I didn't believe in his authority and wouldn't be taking a ticket after all, how do you think that would work out for me? Refusing to acknowledge authority does not exempt you from the consequences of violating authority's laws. Jesus is King, and all the world will answer to Him. Just as important, that gracious, perfect, just, strong warrior King will make right everything that was made wrong when He imposes His perfect will over the earth once and for all. Take heart because Jesus is your King!

DAY 270

JOHN 19:8–16

*R*ead *today's Scripture.* Pilate's torment comes from his refusal to lead. He doesn't want to make what he suspects may be an unethical decision, so he tries to avoid being held responsible for *any* decision in the process. This is despicable for a leader. Leaders must lead. They must be willing to make decisions that do not please people. They must not forsake their own sense of what is right and what is wrong just to be accepted by their followers. As a result, an effective leader is often a lonely man. Boo-hoo. Now, buck up and lead.

Pilate faced Jesus and was impacted by the encounter. Jesus tended to have that effect. Meanwhile, the very people who were pressuring Pilate to put Jesus to death didn't care about Pilate or Roman authority at all. In verse 15, they actually pretended to be loyal to Caesar because they knew this would guilt Pilate into giving them what they wanted. Pilate had power here, but refused to do what was unpopular. That is not leadership. Learn from Pilate's poor example here and be willing to stand by Jesus even if the angry mob tries to manipulate you.

DAY 271

JOHN 19:17–27

Pilate is over it. He has been wrestling with his conscience and forsaking it. He has been pretending as if he's innocent in the ridiculous charade that was Jesus' trial, but he knows that he is the one in authority watching it all happen. He's finally about to successfully resist his own people. Too bad it's over something petty. *Read today's text.*

This mysterious disciple Jesus loved (whose identity will soon be revealed) was there for Jesus when no one else was. All the other disciples and even Jesus' own brothers were nowhere to be found at the moment of His grossly unfair execution. This is probably the reason Jesus delegates His responsibilities as a window's son (Joseph had probably died) to the disciple Jesus loved. Be this disciple. Be the one who refuses to leave your Savior and Friend's side when everyone else falls away and the wolves close in. *Be that man* to someone. Start today by committing to someone, "I want you to know that I'll never leave you." Be willing to follow through with it no matter what. Then, you'll fully understand the Gospel of John.

Day 272

Proverbs 20:5

Men can be private and closed off with their feelings. If you're the kind of guy who feels intensely and out loud and haven't quite learned how to control that yet, then please know *that's okay*. I just want to talk about the way that men can be a little apprehensive about talking the deep stuff. I have another challenge for you, and it flows from *today's verse*.

Translations vary significantly on this verse, but the idea is that men often pack their thoughts and feelings down deep, and it takes someone with tremendous understanding to draw them out. War veterans are often like rugged safes that conceal their violent stories in dark metal chambers. Grown men who still resent their fathers are often like the walking wounded who ignore the arrow sticking straight out of their hearts. Learn from this. Again, fixing your eyes to the horizon of the future and the kind of man you are becoming, I want you to work with your folks to arrange a time for you to meet with an elderly man. Have a deep conversation with him that is based on this question: "What is your story?"

Day 273

Proverbs 20:6-13

The themes of integrity and trustworthiness come roaring back today. *Read today's passage.*

Verses 6 and 7 even use the terms outright, and then verse 11 pounds the concept as if it's a screamo band's pawn-shop drum set. You are known by your actions. Results make you worth hiring/marrying/trusting, and the fruit that is born from your life and faith are far more valuable than the words you use to describe yourself. Evaluate yourself objectively (not with a rigged form of measurement like in verse 10) by taking an inventory of the *results* you produce by the end of the day. Give yourself some physical reminder, like a pen mark, bracelet, or sticky note on your mirror. Tonight, ask yourself, "What did I *produce* today with my actions?" Be real with yourself.

DAY 274

PROVERBS 20:14–21

Did you ever set up a time to have a deep conversation with a trusted elderly man? Again, it's all about having integrity and being trustworthy. Part of being trustworthy is *following through* with what you are asked to do and what you volunteer to do. *Read today's Scripture.*

Verse 14 lets you in on the secret that people will lie to you and try to rip you off, while verse 16 gives the salesman a way to keep from being ripped off ("collateral" is something valuable you leave with a business partner to give him peace of mind that you'll return). So, this passage gives advice to the honorable man living in a dishonorable world.

Take a moment to face this reality: the strong man of God will have a harder time in this life than others but will come out ahead in the end. "An inheritance gained prematurely will not be blessed ultimately" (verse 21). Be ultimately blessed by taking the hard way. Be honorable. Be patient.

HEBREWS 11:3

(A brief apologetics series starts today, beginning with philosophy.)

First Peter 3:15 charged us to be ready to give a reason for our hope. You should be ready to share your testimony and be ready to share the philosophical, scientific, and historical reasoning behind Christianity. This practice of defending Christian reasoning is called "Christian apologetics," and I'm here to equip you with the basics. *Read today's text.*

One of the most basic apologetics is: **"Nothing comes from nothingness, yet we exist. The only way we could come to exist from nothingness** (that's ex nihilo in big-people talk) **is if some nonphysical being or beings created us."** This argument is used against atheism by almost all religions, and it's a devastating argument because there is no answer to it within atheism. Atheists don't know where matter came from. That's step *one*! As far as this argument's use by religions other than Christianity, those religions do *not* have the kind of holy text that we do. We'll get into the specifics of that later. For now, practice explaining this argument (the bold text above), called the "Kalam cosmological argument" to the mirror. This way, you don't mess it up when the time comes to share it.

Day 276

Psalm 14:1

*R*ead *today's verse* and then memorize the basics of Pascal's Wager (paraphrased below):

If God doesn't exist:

- The Christian loses nothing after death and annihilation, but actually gains the benefits of the Christian life, such as peace in times of trouble, an innate sense of purpose in life, fellowship with other believers, and a clear sense of morality.
- The atheist loses the benefits of the Christian life and gains the common pitfalls of the atheistic life, such as a lack of peace, a lack of purpose in existence, and a lack of clarity in what is right or wrong.

If God does exist:

- The Christian gains the benefits of the Christian life *and* spends eternity in heaven with God.
- The atheist not only misses out on the benefits of the Christian life, but also spends eternity in hell apart from God.

The atheist bets eternity in hell (and every other religion's equivalent to hell) that he's right, but realizes he was wrong when it's eternally too late. Atheism isn't worth the risk! This isn't a proof, and a fear of hell doesn't save anyone, but it's important that atheists face this apologetic.

DAY 277

JOB 1:6–12

The problem of evil seems to be the most common reason people have for leaving Christianity. They ask the classic question, "Why does God allow bad things to happen to good people?" The defense of God in response to this question is known as *theodicy. Read today's Scripture.*

Satan is the one responsible for the bad things that happened to Job, but God gave Satan limits that Satan had to respect, and all of it was to prove that Job truly loved God. Satan's accusation in verses 9–11 that Job's love was conditional ended up being proved false over and over again as Job actually praised God after bad things happened. God allows evil to have *some* of its way for now, but He probably does it so that man would be truly free to love God. There is a secret date upon which God will forever destroy evil so that those who believe will spend a perfect eternity with God and without evil forever. Again, rehearse this truth in your own words *right now* so that you will be ready when the time comes.

JOHN 19:28–37

Today we read a tragic, but eternally necessary fulfillment of ancient prophecy. Today, we read about Jesus' death. *Read today's Scripture.*

In verse 30, with His last words, Jesus took your sin to the cross and said, "It is finished!" Your sin is finished! God glorified Himself by, on His own terms, making a way for sinful man to be with Him for eternity. This death took place because *God takes sin seriously!* Everything about the way it happened is also a profound apologetic because, as verified by authoritative sources besides the Bible, this crucifixion was carried out just as Zechariah 12 said it would be centuries upon centuries before crucifixion even existed.

Our sin is finished because of Jesus' sacrifice, and those who believe this will stand before the holy and righteous perfect Judge of the universe with their sins paid for because John 19:30 is true! Go in prayer before God with a heart overflowing with gratefulness because the punishment that brings us peace was upon Jesus in today's text.

JOHN 19:38-42

Do you remember Nicodemus? He's back, and he has come a long way since chapter 3. He is finally ready to defy his fellow Pharisees! He finally has a spine! *Read today's text.*

Once again, we see an apologetic built into this text because we know where this tomb is today! Joseph of Arimathea is a historical figure because he was a rich and prominent guy. Rich and prominent guys tend to leave behind a great deal of artifacts. For example, look at the pyramids of Egypt, the castles of Ireland, and the wealthy ex-wives of Hollywood.

The original Nicodemus did it, and now it's do-it-or-leave-it-alone time for *your* Nicodemus. That's right: dust off the front pages of this book and pray again for your Nicodemus. He is your closet-Christian friend, but today he's in for a rousing pep talk from you about how to become a bold Christian! As you work on what you're going to say, consider whether or not this will be the last pep talk you give him, and consider also . . . if you have lived out the kind of Christian walk that gives you the authority to pep up other Christians. *Oooooh!* Unexpected gut check!

DAY 280

JOHN 20:1–10

Isn't it frustrating to say something important multiple times, but still be ignored? When you say something clearly, but still get the "I don't speak Martian" face, doesn't that make you want to pick up a nearby rabid raccoon and smack this person with it? I do that all the time. *Read today's passage.*

Though Jesus said it several times, the disciples and their friends still didn't get the whole resurrection thing. Mary here is convinced that someone has stolen Jesus' body. Peter and the mystery disciple whom Jesus loved didn't know what to think of it and went back home (verses 9–10). Again, it is one thing to hear Jesus' words, but it is quite another to remember, believe, and act on them when times are hard, as they were for all those mentioned in today's text. Jesus had died! It looked like His being the Messiah was all a big lie or something! The disciples' confusion, by the way, is yet another apologetic: it proves that they didn't steal the body.

Now, there's something Peter noticed in verses 6 and 7 that only makes sense if you understand their culture. People who stepped away from meals temporarily . . . left their napkins folded.

DAY 281

PROVERBS 20:22–30

Redundantly reading references to repetition, *read today's text.*

We have gained momentum on our way through Proverbs, and it is clear that God wants us to know His feelings toward differing weights and dishonest scales, about the splendor of gray hair, and apparently about the value of a good beating. *Ha!* Now, remember this: *something has to be in the Bible only once for it to be God's truth.* So, how much more should we respect those truths that are repeated?

Verse 22 takes immense faith. It's a different kind of faith than the faith you place in your homemade bungee cord. It's faith that is demonstrated through *patience.* Now, connect the truth of verse 22 with the truth of verse 25. Whoa. Don't make a promise you can't keep, especially promised revenge. They will get theirs just like you will get yours. So, in a state of raw prayer before God, let go of all revenge right now. Also, building upon our previous efforts to let our yes be yes and our no be no (James 5:12), be careful not to make commitments you can't keep (verse 25).

DAY 282

PROVERBS 21:1–11

Read today's text. This text reminds me of a man who attended a church I helped out from time to time. He would do the crazy stuff he wanted to (which actually got him shot once) and then would show up again soon after and hand me a sizable check to give to the church as though he were literally paying for his mistakes.

God knows your motives (verse 2 HCSB). He *evaluates* your motives, and that can be scary at times if we're honest. According to this text, instead of giving huge and generous gifts out of sacrifice to the church, God would much rather have had this man just do what was right (verses 2–3). Also according to this text, you're better off living on your roof than inside your house if your wife is a nag! *Bahaha!*

Now, your challenge for this devotional is a big one. In response to verse 11, I want you to teach someone a quick Bible lesson, and that someone has to be wise. Contact a pastor at your church and blame the whole idea on me. *Do it!* According to verse 11, you'll acquire knowledge as a result.

DAY 283

PROVERBS 21:12–19

First John 3:16–18 sets us up for today's text, which is cool because it was written several centuries after Proverbs. This in-our-faces teaching says that we don't have the love of God in us if we close our eyes to the needy when we are able to help them. *Read today's text.*

Verse 13 teaches a similar concept, but with a prophecy. If we shut our ears to the cries of the poor, then we will find ourselves in a place of need with no one to hear our cries. God takes it seriously that those in need be cared for, and He places this responsibility primarily on believers. What a testimony it would be if the people of our churches gave so generously that our whole society would no longer need government-funded programs to care for the poor. Knowing God, your understanding (and especially *my* understanding because I'm a teacher) of this text will soon be tested, so keep your ears open.

Hey, that nagging wife is back again in verse 19. Now her poor husband has moved to the wilderness to get away from her.

DAY 284

GENESIS 1:1–27 (OR AT LEAST 1:1)

Tragically, I don't think the vast majority of creation-theory critics have ever even read the Bible's account of creation. Consider its perfect sense of order and rhythm. Consider how fully comprehensive it is, covering everything from that all-important step one right down to an orderly ecosystem. Consider even its literary beauty and take note of the careful affection with which God creates, lauding each major step for its goodness. This is not only the most comprehensive and evidenced creation theory in existence; it is actually the one and only *complete* theory as to the origins of the universe. There are other creationist accounts, but these are from religious texts of far less historic accuracy than that of the Bible. There are secular accounts, but none of these is complete because all refuse to acknowledge the necessary nonphysical Initiator.

Compare Genesis 1 to how some scientists try to avoid the obvious implication of the Big Bang or to the nonsense of the Theory of Evolution. Note the chaos as matter suddenly makes itself from a violent and disorderly explosion. Note the crass nature of evolutionary theory and the complete lack of fossil evidence for 99 percent of transitional species upon which evolution depends deeply. File all of these facts away in the Apologetics folder of your mind. You're gonna need them!

Day 285

Romans 1:20

Intelligent Design is the common-sense school of thought that looks at the complexity of the universe—from the perfect balance of the planets in orbit down to the mind-blowingly intricate self-sustaining and even self-repairing factories that are our cells—and observes the evidence of design. It is frankly ridiculous to think that such incredible order came about through a series of trillions of accidents with each accident depending on the accident before it. *Read today's text.*

We look at creation and see that it could not have come about through chance and that it bears the fingerprints of a Designer. We have no excuse! Intelligent Design is also not an exclusively Christian argument, but it's a great start. My two favorite teachers in this field are Drs. William Dembski and Michael Behe. They divide Intelligent Design into two ideas: irreducible complexity and specified complexity. Google them.

DAY 286

ISAIAH 40:21–22

Imagine a soldier and his commanding officer. The soldier is slicing his way through a field of thick brush. His commanding officer is watching him from overhead in helicopter. The commanding officer can see where his soldier has been and where he is going. The soldier is able to disobey the orders from his commanding officer, but that wouldn't be wise, would it? It would not because the commanding officer can see things the soldier cannot. *Read today's Scripture.*

We perceive time as it ticks by in seconds and minutes. However, God is free from the chains of the clock. He currently exists at the beginning and the end simultaneously (Revelation 1:8; 21:6; 22:13). He sees what is ahead of us. He is enthroned above the earth and has been there since the beginning. This attribute of God, that He has no beginning and no end, is what makes the existence of matter possible. Physical matter cannot create itself out of nothingness, yet here we are. This is only possible because God, who has no beginning, began the earth. Consider the foundations, the very beginning, of the earth. God is your commanding officer. You are His soldier on the ground.

DAY 287

JOHN 20:11–16

Straight up, if I saw a couple of angels, I would probably need to change my pants. Mary Magdalene, however, sees a couple of angels, seems unimpressed, *still doesn't get the resurrection thing*, and has a quick chat with someOne whom she thinks is the gardener. *Read today's text.*

In our times of lostness and confusion, God is at work. Though we don't recognize His handiwork and mistake it for something or someone else, He is in control and moving on our behalf. In tears, we may think that God is nowhere to be found, just like Mary Magdalene thought here, but Jesus is alive. Before you think you've been abandoned by God, take a second look at what's happening in your life. God calls you by name.

DAY 288

JOHN 20:17–18

Read today's text. At times during Jesus' life before the crucifixion, it seemed that He was distant toward His followers who didn't believe in Him. He would leave them hanging and encourage others to do the same if necessary (Matthew 12:46–50 and Mark 10:29–30). But they are the first people on His mind after the resurrection, according to John's gospel. He even broke away from Mary Magdalene's hug to send her to them! He sent word to them that He was going to be with His heavenly Father and with your Father (verse 17).

Jesus is alive, and you are on His heart! Even those who are far from God and those who reject Jesus for a time and to an extent can be radically saved. We have essentially just read what led to the salvation of James, whose book we've studied in this devotional! Though His brothers mocked Jesus before (John 7:1–9), they end up becoming powerful praying believers (Acts 1:14). Let your heart be filled with ambitious hope that those in your life who now mock God may one day become evangelists in Jesus' name! I think it's time for some ambitious evangelism starting *today*.

John 20:19–31

Read today's passage. The resurrected Jesus just shows up and crashes the party! The disciples were all cowering behind their locked doors because of the violence awaiting them outside, and Jesus meets them right there in their fear, says, "Peace to you," and then commissions them with His breath of the Holy Spirit. They tell Thomas repeatedly, and Jesus gives him eight days to come around. (This is why he's called "Doubting Thomas.") Verse 29 is about *you*, my reader, and you are more blessed than Thomas because you believe without seeing, whereas Thomas missed the opportunity to show great faith by believing without seeing.

As we go through this season of studying apologetics, share verses 29–31 with the Thomases in your life, those people whose faith is so weak it is dependent upon physical proof. Tell them they are missing the opportunity to show faith and are missing out on a blessing!

DAY 290

PROVERBS 21:20–31

Wow! Our passage in Proverbs today is once again *packed* with wisdom worth more than gold. *Read verse 20 and keep your finger on it.* Verse 20 builds upon the second half of verse 17. The cost of abusing alcohol, cigarettes, junk food, video games, and anything whose sole purpose is pleasure and nothing productive really adds up, and after you've consumed these products, you have nothing to show but a skinnier bank balance and a good time gone by—unless, of course, you get lung cancer . . . then it's . . . sort of like you have something to show for your cigarettes. *Sheesh.*

Then, building on that point, *read verses 25 and 26* and consider the slacker's torment to be filled with cravings and never satisfied. *It's easier to do the work.* Then, like the righteous man in verse 26, you can give generously (remember: we want to known as generous men) without holding back. Don't you love the guy who doesn't hold back when he gives? *You could be him!*

Read the rest and see the futility of the brilliant men who strive to disprove God's existence. Be confident as you stand in defense of the faith. No atheist's education will prevail against God (verse 30).

DAY 291

PROVERBS 22:1–9

*R*ead today's text. Let's talk *money*, yo! The Bible has much to say about your finances because your finances are a tremendous indicator of what's going on in your heart. We'll talk tithing later, but first let's talk *debt*. There is an extremely good chance that most of your friends are going to go into debt, meaning that they will owe people more money than they have. You can go into debt by financing a car, by taking out a student loan, by not paying your taxes (yikes!), and just by spending more than you should by bustin' out the magic plastic we call a "credit card." People also go into debt because of things that are beyond their control, though. My family was in medical debt for a while, for example, because we had to pay off Aiden's medical bills.

Let's combine verses 6 and 7 right now and decide that you will *not* get into debt so that you will never owe money (except for a mortgage to buy a house one day) and therefore never be a "slave."

Day 292

Proverbs 22:10–23

The first verse you're going to read today is the best advice on the planet for leaders. If you're in a leadership role in some sort of team or organization and have that one person who is just smack in the middle of all the strife and drama, he or she is not going to like verse 10. But you're going to love it if you have the authority to follow through with it. The famous football coach Lou Holtz once said, "Motivation is simple: you eliminate those who are not motivated." *Read today's Scripture.*

We have just entered a phase of Proverbs wherein the wise and experienced veteran with godly wisdom is going to give us what we could never give ourselves. It's not likely that the future Jesse at the end of my life will be able to come back in time to tell the present Jesse everything he's learned, but at least I can read this new section of Proverbs!

Our challenge today comes from the humorous verse 13. Slackers have plenty of excuses, so today you will make absolutely no excuses whatsoever. Go!

DAY 293

ISAIAH 66:8

Back to apologetics, today you're going to get up from your devotional equipped with a powerful proof of the Bible, an undeniable fulfillment of biblical prophecy that is so ridiculously verifiable, it's probably in the news today. The nation of Israel, sometimes named by the flexible term *Zion* in the Bible, was utterly annihilated in the year AD 70, just as Jesus said it would be in Matthew 24. The people of Israel scattered, their language declined, their military disappeared, and their nation no longer existed. Then, after World War II ended the Holocaust (which was also prophesied in Ezekiel 37), Israel came back into existence as a nation on *May 14, 1948*! *Read today's verse*.

Almost 1,900 years after it was erased from the face of the earth, Israel returned just as prophesied in a mind-blowing event that has never happened before or since. Countries don't just come back into existence, my student, and this was all prophesied in Ezekiel 36:22–24; Ezekiel 37:1, 11–14; Ezekiel 38:8, 12; Jeremiah 16:14–15; Jeremiah 31:3–9; Amos 9:11–15; Acts 1:6–7; and Isaiah 66:8–9. You are now armed and dangerous.

DAY 294

ISAIAH 53:6

*R*ead today's verse and then name the person about whom its words *are written.* Who is the "him" in this verse? Ask anyone: it's obviously Jesus. Now, here's the thing: this book is archaeologically verified to have been written eight hundred years before Jesus' birth! Other ancient messianic (having to do with our Savior the Messiah) prophecies fulfilled include Micah 5:2; Joshua 19:15–16; Isaiah 9:1–2; and Micah 4:1–3. Mark this page for all the fulfilled prophetic Scripture references in this devotional and the previous one.

The Bible's history is airtight and even ahead of archaeology. Entire people groups, historic locations, and prominent individuals mentioned in the Bible and only the Bible were dismissed by atheists for a lack of artifact evidence for decades. Prominent atheists like Sir William Ramsay of Oxford University even set out on expeditions to disprove books of the Bible, like Acts, but ended up finding evidence of the Bible's claims and becoming Christians themselves!

No historical discovery has ever disproven the Bible, but only backed it up further. It's the most consistent, copied, and well-preserved ancient document in the world by a devastating margin. It's trustworthy; therefore, so are its beautiful promises of hope!

Day 295

ACTS 9:1–9, THEN 17–20

In Acts 7 (which we'll study soon) this guy Saul from Tarsus, who was like a Pharisee on steroids, oversaw the first martyrdom of the new covenant recorded in Scripture as he approved of Stephen's execution. He went on from there with authority to arrest followers of "the Way," and that's where we pick up the story. *Read both passages of today's text.*

This is pretty much the ultimate testimony, but *you* have one that is just as powerful. Your testimony is your salvation story. Sure, some people have these crazy testimonies about how they used to be crack-addicted cannibals before they became vegan missionaries to Ethiopian orphans, but the same Holy Spirit that gives power to Saul's testimony gives power to yours. This is the best apologetic because you're the world's expert at it, and you know that no monkey skull they dig up will ever change what God has done in your life! I see radical transformations in people's lives all the time, and each story is an undeniable proof of God. Share yours today.

DAY 296

JOHN 21:20–25

(We already read verses 1–19 in our study of Peter's life.)

Today, we finish something we started on Day 240! Way to finish what you start, bro! That's part of being the honorable and trustworthy man described in Proverbs. That's part of being a strong man of God. Following through with what you start is *hugely* important in your professional life and especially in your future marriage. This text picks up right after the breakfast on the beach where Jesus restores Peter by three times questioning his love and then commissioning him. Brace yourself: the identity of the mystery disciple whom Jesus loved is about to be revealed! *Read today's Scripture.*

Awww, snapdragons! You didn't see that coming, did you? (That is, unless you've read another Gospel.) It was *John,* this Gospel's author all along! He was referring to himself as "the disciple Jesus loved" because he knew Jesus loved him. Jesus' love for him became his defining characteristic: it became his identity. So, we finish this Gospel where we started it, where we started this devotional book together. Who are you? You are loved by God. That is a *powerful* basis for an identity. Let it be yours.

DAY 297

PROVERBS 22:24–29

I was raised in a country-boy lifestyle—going to rodeos every weekend, riding horses, fishing, and taking the four-wheeler to the creek in the woods to catch crayfish with my cousins. Many of my family members speak with a Southern accent, but I have pretty much lost mine over the years . . . though it does return when I spend time with Southern folks. Without realizing it, we tend to speak and act like those around us (even influential-leader types), and that's not always a good thing (verse 25). *Read today's Scripture.*

I love verse 29's application for your circumstances. At your phase of life, you stand at an all-you-can-attempt buffet of opportunities. You can be involved in three sports at once and take on a double major while being in student government. I know how it is: I was involved in everything I could be involved in and tend to drift back into that tendency today (which isn't good for a family man). The man in verse 29, however, specializes. He focuses. He is skilled because he had a head start, developing a profitable skill since his youth. Be a man of focus today.

DAY 298

PROVERBS 23:1–11

Please, start today by praying for your Pharisees. Lift them up before God and pray that you would be given the immense honor of sharing the true gospel with them. *Read today's Scripture.*

This is the most amazing book of wisdom on the planet. I've just been sitting here with my wife marveling at how perfect and priceless these words are. Notice the contrasting, yet similar themes of verses 1–3 and 6–8. Watch yourself when eating with royalty and watch yourself when eating with a stingy person. Let's hope that these meals aren't one in the same too! Ha!

Write verses 4 and 5 on your arm. Wow, what a countercultural (meaning it's against what society does) way of thinking about wealth. Wealth can disappear in an instant. I've seen fabulously rich people lose it all in the housing bubble. Though I'm not a wealthy man, I lost money, too, and it had nothing to do with my decisions! It just happened! So, stay out of debt, develop a profitable skill, do what you love if you can, but don't kill yourself to get rich.

DAY 299

PROVERBS 23:12–25

As a father of boys, I ache to experience verse 24 realized in my own sons. *Read today's Scripture.*

Verses 19–21 address drunkenness, which we've discussed before, but they also address something we haven't yet, and that is gluttony. Gluttony is essentially overeating, but it's about more than food. Now, don't tune me out just because you *currently* have the metabolism of a caffeinated cheetah. There was a time I, too, could eat an entire raw bison for lunch, but those days are gone for me as they will be for you, so *listen.* It is one thing to lack the self-control necessary to stop doing something that is pleasurable, such as the case when eating after you're full, but gluttony also reveals a failure to see the goodness of *enough.* So, today in food and in everything that is good, be grateful for enough and learn the peace that comes from being satisfied. Be satisfied today, my student, not gluttonous.

Day 300

Proverbs 23:26-35

Check in on your Philip, Andrew, and (I hope) Peter right now. Send them a quick uplifting text or make plans to hang out, and then *read today's text*.

Verses 29–35 paint vivid imagery of a destroyed and foolish man whose insatiable god is wine. I know such men. I have seen them lose scholarships and opportunities because, ironically, *they* were consumed by alcohol.

Verses 26–28 bring us back to adulterous women and pornography. Have you kept yourself pure? Have you guarded your own heart? You know, your heart and body don't belong only to you. They also belong to your future wife if it's God's will that you be married one day. Getting caught up in things with women who compromise your purity is like falling into a deep pit or down a narrow well. It's like getting caught up in an ambush or hit by a robber. Those experiences *steal* from you and your possible future bride. Go back to good old Psalm 51 as a prayer of repentance.

DAY 301

PROVERBS 24:1–12

Get acquainted with feeling left out sometimes because of your faith. Sorry, I know that's not a happy injection of bunny dreams and rainbow sprinkles, but it's true. If you're being bold and forthright about your faith (not arrogant and condescending, mind you), then your presence will make people uncomfortable when they're up to something that they know doesn't align with Christian values or the Christian worldview. Don't forsake your convictions to be accepted. Remember Pilate? Don't pout when it happens. Don't be a jerk. Play it cool and know that this minor sense of rejection is a hint at persecution and that you are blessed because of it! Don't relent. Don't envy evil men. Be who you are and be willing to stand alone. *Read today's Scripture.*

Similarly, verses 10–12 show that we won't be able to claim ignorance before God when we see people heading for destruction, but attempt nothing. Today, verse 11 is your mission. As Ephesians 2:10 teaches, God prepares in advance opportunities for us to do good things, so be on the lookout for that hurting person. Be willing to speak to the one who is in self-destruct mode even if you speak alone.

DAY 302

PROVERBS 24:13–25

I eat straight honey. I just upend the little plastic bear and unleash the glory. It's amazing. My parents have a couple of beehives (which I used to kick and then sprint away from), and harvesting the honey is a cool/nerve-racking/delicious experience. *Read today's text* and feel the way about wisdom the way I do about honey. Remember John the Baptist and his wild honey—possibly bees, stingers, honeycomb, and all?

Building on yesterday's call not to envy evil men, don't throw a party in your head when those who reject you stumble and fall. Verse 18 is fascinating to me because it teaches that God will actually spare an evil person His wrath because of the way a Christian responds to it. I wonder how many people didn't reap the punishment they sowed in scheming because the Christians in their lives reveled in their enemies' humiliation.

DAY 303

ACTS 1:4–11

(New Series: Action-Packed Highlight Reel of the Book of Acts)

So, now that we've finished the Gospel of John, what happened to the disciples? Luke describes a great deal of it in this *massive* letter to a guy named (get this) Theophilus. This is the beginnings of the church, and the events of the book of Acts are still resonating today. In fact, you're reading this book because the Acts happened. We jump in with one of the most amazing events in Jesus' ministry, and that is His ascension into heaven. *Read today's Scripture.*

In verse 6, the disciples were expecting the Second Coming right away, and even then they thought it would be political in nature. They thought Jesus would now kick the Romans out of Israel. Jesus' answer in verse 8 is epic, and its challenge applies to you today. Filled with the Holy Spirit, be a witness to others about Jesus all over the place, starting with right where you are. Go on mission both at home and abroad. Is it God's will that you go on mission? *Yes!* I know this because I can read Acts 1:8 and Matthew 28:18–20! Go now because, just as the angels said in verse 11, Jesus is coming back!

DAY 304

ACTS 3:1–10

After Peter's big jump-start of the church at Pentecost in Acts 2 (when three thousand people were saved), the Holy Spirit filled the disciples, and they were, exactly as Jesus prophesied, able to do even more amazing miracles than what Jesus did. *Read today's passage.*

I love the healed man in this passage. He's loud and bold. He's disorderly. He is leaping as he praises God (verse 8). Do you remember when you were still soaking wet from the baptistery (if you haven't been baptized, by the way, call your church and schedule that today) and you were an evangelism volcano? Take a moment right now and, as God spoke to the church of Ephesus in Revelation 2, remember the height from which you have fallen. Do the things you did when you were just raised to walk as a Christian. Be disorderly today in the way you evangelize. Go jump and cause a ruckus.

DAY 305

ACTS 4:1–20
(If you can bring yourself to stop reading!)

Our own Peter and John team up and crack some skulls today. In the aftershock of this forty-year-old man being healed, they stand before a fierce counsel of the most brilliant and educated men in all of Israel—and by the power of the Holy Spirit *boldly* defy them. *Read today's Scripture.*

Peter and John, as you know, didn't have master's degrees, but they had the Holy Spirit, and the man they had healed stood right there next to them. You can't deny results! Can you point to the results in your evangelism walk? Write verse 20 somewhere. Put it on your locker, your hand, your mirror (I know chicks usually do that, but it's cool), or wherever you'll see it. Approach this day from the spirit in which you *cannot* stop speaking about Jesus.

Day 306

Proverbs 24:26–34

Read today's Scripture. Today, go around kissing everyone right on the lips . . . verse 26-style, that is. Be honest.

Verse 27 is bigger than housework. It's a call to do the hard work that pays the bills before you do the work you really want to do. Finish your homework, cut the grass, wash the dishes, finish your shift; *then* wax your surfboard. You'll better enjoy the fun stuff without the lame stuff hanging over your head. It's about follow-through, remember?

That flows perfectly into the famous verses 30–34 that teach a vivid lesson on the dangers of laziness. Hitting the hay instead of staying up as long as it takes to finish an assignment is so tempting. Hitting the snooze button instead of getting to class on time is *so* easy. These, however, are the habits of a man who is poor without excuse. *Not* you, my student. Do the work, the work that matters, and set yourself up to pass the competition when it counts. We live in a competitive society, and I've seen people smarter and more talented than I am eat my dust, and it's all because they didn't wake up for class. That will *not* be you.

DAY 307

PROVERBS 25:1–7

Judah had its share of lousy and ungodly kings, but Hezekiah was a strong man of God. He compiled these pieces of wisdom from Solomon because, according to 2 Chronicles 31:21, he sought after God's laws with all of his heart (KJV). So, the very existence of the next five chapters proves 2 Chronicles 31:21. *Read today's text.*

Verses 6 and 7 contain a lesson that people are likely to learn the hard way. Be realistic about your own prominence and influence. Don't help yourself to an honor you have not earned, and spare yourself the humiliation of publicly overestimating your standing with someone of importance. It is far better to be invited up than awkwardly put down.

Jesus actually taught this proverb in parable form in Luke 14:7–11, and with it He gave this powerful truth: "Everyone who exalts himself will be humbled, and the one who humbles himself will be exalted" (verse 11). Today, I want you to humble yourself. I want you to downplay yourself. The overly proud man will be humbled either on his own terms and by his own voluntary words or by the bursting of his delusional bubble and disciplining from the God who opposes the proud.

DAY 308

PROVERBS 25:8–17

Read today's text. The first of the three sections we'll focus on today (again, though, be sensitive to the Holy Spirit's potential leading to focus on another section) is the call to handle conflict privately, found in verses 8–10. Apply this to social media and handle awkward confrontations in a private way, preferably the good, old-fashioned face-to-face, but at the very least not in an online forum that the world can see and save.

Verses 11–12 give us our challenge for the day. A man can have all the wisdom in the world, but if he has the worst sense of timing imaginable, then his wisdom is wasted. I once enthusiastically shared with my wife about the way I lost five pounds in a week. She was pregnant at the time, so it didn't go over well. Timing, my student, timing.

Tertiarily (lay that one on the third body paragraph of your next paper—*BOOM*), verses 16 and 17 bring our attention to the possibility that we might smother people and outstay our welcome. Even as a lover of honey, I know this one's a real possibility, so heads up!

DAY 309

ACTS 5:17–32

Peter's comeback from denying Jesus and cowering at the accusations of little girls has been roaring since Acts 2, where he led thousands of people to Christ. Can you imagine leading a bunch of nonbelievers to faith in Christ and producing an entire megachurch in a single day? Well, he's not slowing down. He and our boys like John have gone from hiding behind their locked doors in the final chapters of John's Gospel to preaching loudly in the most public place possible—Solomon's Colonnade. How cool is it that this colonnade in which our own authors Peter and John are preaching is named after our other author, the author of Proverbs, Solomon? *Read today's Scripture.*

They were busted out of jail by an angel and then went right back to the place they were arrested and kept on preaching. How righteously defiant! Have hostile people tried to silence your evangelistic efforts? I hope you're that vocal about your faith. Don't shove it down the throats of those who just won't hear it (remember the rocky soil?), but *definitely* don't back down when the enemy uses people to silence you.

ACTS 7:51–60

Many of the people in the New Testament (including earthly Bible authors) knew the Old Testament. They contributed to the Bible having known the Bible, and the same Holy Spirit was at work in every generation of earthly biblical authors from Moses several millennia ago to John in the first century AD. In Acts 7, Stephen schools the high priest on the ancient history of Israel and calls the Jewish leaders out straight to their faces. It's a brilliant and passionate discourse. It results in his death. *Read today's Scripture.*

There are important theological (the study of God) and soteriological (the study of how people are saved) implications to verse 51, which I do want you to meditate on later, but today let's focus on Stephen. He prayed for those who stoned him to death *as* they were stoning him to death. He asked God not to "hold this sin against them" as he received a standing ovation from Jesus (verse 55). Meanwhile, Saul of Tarsus watched approvingly. Pray a Stephen-style prayer for your Pharisees right now.

DAY 311

ACTS 8:4–13

Stephen's execution was intended for evil, but God used it for good. The hateful men who covered their ears and shouted as Stephen spoke the truth of God thought they were victorious, but only spread Christianity. (Funny, an atheist I know once drew a picture of Christians doing that, without realizing he was drawing the nonbelievers of Acts 7.) Believers preached the gospel as they fled (verse 4). *Read today's passage.*

Your God is more powerful than the darkness. He has overcome the world. I have seen people just like the former sorcerer Simon in today's text come to Christianity from Satanism and other pagan religions. Do you know someone of a false faith? If so, don't you dare get up from your seat until you have prayerfully come to the place in your heart where you genuinely believe that you could realistically lead that person to Christ. Using your imagination, envision that person standing next to you in worship singing out to God. Let this vision be a wordless prayer. Believe this vision is possible. That person's eternity could depend on it.

DAY 312

PROVERBS 25:18–28

Here's a quick chemistry lesson on verse 20: natron (or "soda") is a naturally occurring, chunky, baking soda–like substance. The CSB, ESV, and NASB use the original Hebrew term for what we call "soda" here, but the NIV, *The Message*, and the NLT convey the same message with different words. The idea of verse 20 is that someone with a heavy heart would find it irritating or even painful if you were to try to cheer him up with a light and fluffy song. *Read today's Scripture.*

Verses 21 and 22 combine with verse 26 to give us our challenge for today. Verse 26 is about standing your ground and refusing to back down from God's standards. As soon as you back off and give in to peer pressure to do something contrary to the Bible, you send mixed messages that could throw people off their progress toward God. However, verses 21 and 22 tell us to be kind to our enemies, and it's possible that "the wicked" (verse 26) could also be "your enemy" (verses 21 and 22). Give an encouraging word to your enemy today. May they know you stand in disagreement with them, but still be blessed by you.

DAY 313

PROVERBS 26:1–12

Read today's text. The first time I read this, when I was your age, I was thinking all the way through verse 11, *Yeah, take that, fool! I'm so glad that I'm smart.* Every one of those verses just pummels the fool. Then I arrived at verse 12 and saw that, because I thought I was so smart, *I was worse off than the fool!*

It's incredibly difficult to have a realistic view of one's own intelligence. Men can be especially prone to pride, which makes us overestimate ourselves. At the same time, report cards and standardized test scores don't always paint an accurate picture of who is smarter than whom. I'd like to say I learned this lesson the easy way, by reading verse 12, but I didn't. I learned it the hard way, by running my mouth to those who actually knew what they were talking about . . . when I didn't. I made a fool of myself because I thought I was wise.

One of life's most important lessons to learn (and hopefully learn only once) is to be aware of how little you actually know. Never believe that you have learned enough. Be *ever* hungry for wisdom.

Day 314

Proverbs 26:13–16

To build on yesterday's message, I think it's time for some more floor pounding. It's been a while since we first pounded the floor and asked God for wisdom. Start today's devotional off by waking up the people downstairs—and yes, I'm serious. Don't forget James 1:5-8 as you do. *Then, read today's Scripture.*

When I was in college, I was the captain of the drumline at FSU. A friend of my girlfriend's introduced me to her little brother, who had idolized the drumline his whole life and told me about how nervous he was for the upcoming tryouts. I gave him some pointers and told him exactly how to prepare. A few months later, I found him buried deep in the crowd of his fellow rookie candidates, and he seemed as cocky as could be. After the first round of auditions, though, he looked like a whipped puppy. He was lazy and hadn't prepared, though I had told him everything he needed to know months in advance. He was the slacker in these verses, and his excuses were almost as ridiculous. He hung his head because he knew he had blown the opportunity to live his dream.

Learn from him.

DAY 315

ACTS 8:26–40

Read today's Scripture. I love Philip's no-questions-asked obedience to *whatever* God tells him to do as he spreads the gospel. This desert road to Gaza was an empty no-man's land, but Philip says, "Sure, God." The Holy Spirit tells him to approach some random chariot, and he *runs* up to it (verse 30). "Sure, God." He explains the gospel, spots a random oasis in the desert (which I think God may have created just for this), and baptizes the guy before being miraculously teleported to another city. "Sure, God," he says and then immediately evangelizes more. I *love* that!

Now, imagine this from the Ethiopian's perspective. You spent some serious cash on a prophecy that you don't understand, and as you're puzzling over it, some random guy shows up sprinting next to your chariot window and asks, "Do you understand what you're reading?" Ha! God is so awesome!

When I last preached this passage, one of our other pastors came in to briefly interrupt, and without knowing what we were studying, introduced our newest pastor . . . who was from Africa! Again, God is so awesome!

Evangelize just like Philip. Today, to whatever the Spirit asks of you, say, "Sure, God."

DAY 316

ACTS 14:8–20

Yesterday, my son Asher took his first steps! My wife and I were ecstatic, but Asher was probably happier than us about it. In today's text, we meet a man who never took a step in his life until he encountered the Holy Spirit of God. *Read today's text.*

It is inflammatory to call out to a man who has never been able to walk, "Stand up on your feet!" Yet, Paul said it, and it took faith to do so. He could see in the man's eyes that he had faith.

Don't stop at just the Andrew and Philip in your life when it comes to evangelism. I hope that you have seen many others come to faith in Christ by now. Either way, today I want you to call someone out of his spiritually crippled state. It takes faith because you could get shot down, but you could also see someone's first steps—steps of faith toward Jesus as the Holy Spirit draws him. If you get shot down, then do what Paul does in verses 19 and 20: he got up and went *back* into the city that just stoned him!

DAY 317

ACTS 16:5

As a strong man of God, I hope that you take as much ownership as is appropriate over the health of your church. Be a part of your parents' church or bring your parents to church with you. Even if your church has only a halfway decent ministry for you, then become an active participant and fan of it because *our churches need men*! It's not just your minister's job to grow your church. *It's your job too!* So, how do you help grow your church? *Read today's verse.*

Imagine that: the church grew in number *as* it grew in faith. Step out in faith and invite someone to go to church with you today!

Now, I realize that sometimes Christians may need to find a new church. If that's been on your heart for a while and you understand that any church you switch to will have problems of its own, then prayerfully seek wise counsel and consider speaking with your minister before moving to another church. Realize the problem may lie with *you* and not the church. Either way, once you've stepped on board with a good church, grab an oar and start rowing!

DAY 318

PROVERBS 26:17

My wife and I spent this past week in Jamaica. The island has about as many dogs as it has palm trees! In the ancient Hebrew culture in which this text was originally written, dogs were considered unclean animals. With that in mind, *read today's verse*.

I've always been that guy who would follow up on a dare (I've chugged more than my share of hot sauce and jumped off a thirty-plus-foot cliff into the ocean three times in Jamaica last week), but I would *never* grab a random dog by the ears if someone dared me to. That's what it's like to step into someone else's argument. Stay clear of the drama both in person and online.

DAY 319

PROVERBS 26:18–28

Men joke. We slam each other, punch each other, and prank our best friends sometimes. It's somehow meant to be funny. I get this kind of humor, and I do think it can be genuinely hilarious when done right, but I have also seen it stir up anger and end in unbearable awkwardness or even woundedness. Cowards sometimes use this form of joking to express their thinly veiled hostility or jealousy. They'll say something terrible, but say it with a smile and finish it with a loud laugh, pretending they're joking. With their smiles and with their forced laughter, they lie. These verse-19 jokers are the subject of *today's text*.

Take a minute to catalogue your most recent jokes on people. Do so by envisioning yourself saying them from the perspective of those who heard them. Do your jokes pass the Proverbs 26 test?

Now, what about jokes made at your expense? Most of the time, you have to keep in mind that it's just a joke and come up with a way to joke right back. However, if you suspect that someone's jokes are actually bullying, then consider confronting him *privately*. He'll likely back down.

DAY 320

PROVERBS 27:1

On any night in my high-school career, you could have smacked me in the face with a wet squid to wake me up and asked me what I was doing with my life, and I would have instantly told you I was going to be a mechanical engineer. Then I would have asked you why you just hit me with a squid. Seriously, why? Anyway, I was completely wrong. I had a detailed life plan. I gobbled up all the college courses I could while I was in high school so that I could try to graduate early and start to work for the company I had chosen. Today, I'm a pastor and professional drummer. Funny, huh? *Read today's verse.*

It is great to have a sense of direction for your life, but you *must* be willing to let God alter that direction even if it's into something radical and scary. Do not drift aimlessly, but also do not bulldoze through the Spirit's leading in your life. Just as we learned in James 4:13–16, your will for your future should be subject to God's will first. As this verse cautions, speak carefully about your future.

DAY 321

ACTS 16:6–10

Speaking of finding God's will for your life, here is that aforementioned passage in which God directly intervenes twice to redirect Paul and his bros. *Read today's Scripture.*

I have something amazing to tell you. God is still doing this kind of thing today. Missionaries overseas have independently from one another reported visions leading them to fruitful evangelistic endeavors. Think about the ramifications of that. Think about what that means. God is still doing today the amazing things He did throughout the book of Acts! Close your eyes and pray now for all those people groups who need the gospel, but have never heard it. Pray for the millions of people within the "10/40 Window." That is the land between 10 and 40 degrees latitude between northern Africa and southern Asia. As you can see on the International Mission Board's annual map entitled "The Global Status of Evangelical Christianity," that is the part of the world that most needs the gospel, and those people need your prayers right now.

If you want to pray specifically, check out *Operation World* by Jason Mandryk. It's full of information on each country's spiritual status.

DAY 322

ACTS 16:25–34

Surgeons were rushed in to save Aiden's life after he was born. I tried hard to keep myself together for my wife. As the doctors operated on our boy, I sat next to my bride on her tiny hospital bed, held her hands, and the two of us began to worship God together. It was the darkest hour of our lives. *Read today's Scripture.*

As they're wrongfully imprisoned, Paul and Silas worshipped God. As they worshipped, a violent earthquake shook the prison's foundations, their prison doors flew open, and their chains fell off (verse 26). In the darkest hour of night, about midnight (verse 25), they praised God, and God showed up in a huge way that led to the salvation not only of the prison guard, but his family as well (verses 33–34).

As Jessi and I sang, our door opened too. It was our surgeons who said, "We cannot explain why your son is alive. It is a miracle." I looked up to heaven, but noticed the clock: it was midnight, and I was to preach this chapter the next day. In your darkest hour of night, worship until the walls fall down and your chains come off!

DAY 323

ACTS 17:22–34

(or verses 16–34 if you have time)

*R*ead *today's text.* Paul was grieved over the fact that this city's people were worshipping so many different gods that they even built an altar to one they may have missed (verses 16 and 23)! So, he *uses* that altar "to an unknown god" to show them that they had indeed missed One, and that One was the One true God! Notice how he studied what they believed (verse 23) and spoke with them on terms they understood. Paul connected with lost people right where they were and used what they knew and believed to bring them to the gospel. He was an incredibly effective evangelist to say the least, and much of that is because of this connection he made with those he evangelized.

In 1 Corinthians 9:19–23, Paul writes about how he did whatever it took and became whatever it took by all means possible so that some might be saved. Likewise, without giving a false impression about your beliefs, establish a connection with someone who is far from the gospel and base that connection on what you have in common and what you understand about his beliefs. Listen genuinely. Then, seeing eye-to-eye, walk him to the gospel.

Day 324

Proverbs 27:2-6

It is time for another pride checkup. If your phone has the technical capacity and battery life for it, consider using a sound recording app to record your interactions today. If you can't do that, then give yourself some sort of physical reminder to make you think about being recorded, like wearing your watch on the opposite wrist, drawing a mic on your hand, or programming a calendar reminder. It's important not to share these recordings, but to listen to the way you talk. If you forget that you're being recorded, you'll get an authentic sample of how you speak. If you find yourself *changing* the way you speak, then write in your journal exactly *what* you changed and *why*. *Read today's Scripture*.

At the end of the day, see if your speech passed the Proverbs 27:2 test. Did you brag or even say something deliberately to cast yourself in a favorable light? "Today in weightlifting as I was benching 950, Juan said the funniest thing. . . ." This is sometimes called "backdoor bragging," and I was the champ at it. We are to let *others* compliment us, and they can't do that if we take every opportunity to compliment ourselves.

DAY 325

PROVERBS 27:7–16

Read verse 7. We so often don't know what we have until we lose it. We can take for granted the good things that become routine to us. For instance, since returning from my last mission trip, I am *incredibly* grateful for air-conditioning, yet never once thanked God for air-conditioning before that trip. Take inventory of the overlooked honeycomb in your life. Today, you will begin a "fast" from certain luxuries in your life so that you might become hungry for them and therefore grateful for them.

Read the rest of today's text. The one in verse 14 who compliments his neighbor before he could do anything worth complimenting is probably using flattery. Let your compliments be authentic and not some way to manipulate (control) people.

Verses 15 and 16 are bad news. In the same way that you can't control the wind or grab oil, you can't control a nagging wife! If even Solomon, who had godly wisdom poured out on him, could not control a nagging wife, then neither can we. Keep that in mind as you ready yourself for marriage, no matter how far over the horizon it may now seem.

PROVERBS 27:17

Did you do the recording thing, and have you started your "fast" from yesterday's devotional? If not, write a note in your calendar to start because I have *another* challenge for you today. *Read today's verse*.

Imagine two pieces of iron colliding. Hear the sound upon impact and see the resulting sparks fly. Both pieces are sharper now. You need other men in your life to hold you accountable, men with whom you can collide to be mutually sharpened. Think about the other strong men (accountability needs to be gender-focused) of God at your church, and go up to *at least* one this week (or send a message right now) to start some structured accountability time. Church buddies are great because you already see them weekly.

Here's your group's routine: you go around the group to quickly follow up from your last meeting and then lay out new things to confess, goals to set, or situations to pray about. You pray, and you move on to the next man. That's it. Also, do your research and find a suitable online accountability software that would report each man's fishy online activity to the others in the group. Be struck and sharpened. Strike to sharpen others.

DAY 327

ACTS 18:5–8

*R*ead today's text. We all have that line we won't cross when it comes to pressing forward with an evangelistic conversation. For some it's the moment when the conversation becomes remotely awkward. For Paul the apostle, it was when they became blasphemous (meaning they hated the Holy Spirit and thought He was evil) or started stoning him to death. *Remember this:* Paul led more people to Christ than the average Christian in part because Paul's line was way beyond that of the average Christian. I think it's time for a little (don't take this the wrong way) "offensive" evangelism that pushes the line out of where we're comfortable and into the realm of where God wants it. It's time to evangelize not in proportion to what we feel okay doing, but in proportion to what God is able to do!

After getting shot down, Paul just goes one door over, and an entire family is saved, followed by many more people in the city! Push the line past where you're comfortable in evangelism and don't give up if you get shot down. You're closer than you think. Just go one "door" down, and you might see revival start!

ACTS 18:24–28

*R*ead today's Scripture. First off, I love this husband and wife Aquila and Priscilla, and it's not just because I like it when spouses' names rhyme. I love that every time one of them is named in the Bible, the other one is named too. They did ministry as a couple. Think on this, too, as you prepare for marriage one day.

Now, Apollos was preaching an incomplete gospel. Remember John the Baptist baptizing people in repentance for their sins as a way to prepare for the Messiah's arrival? Apollos was still preaching *that* way, as though Jesus had not yet come. He was from the city of Alexandria (of which there were two), which was full of sketchy theology. Priscilla and Aquila, however, saw what a passionate and clearly gifted speaker he was (verses 24 and 25), trained him correctly (verse 26), and then watched him go (verses 27 and 28). You will encounter other Christians who have different theologies from you. They may have some things confused. Do you know anyone like Apollos who is clearly gifted, but theologically misguided? Pray now that God would do in his or her life what He did in Apollos's life.

DAY 329

ACTS 27:9–12

At this point, the imprisoned Paul has been an apostle pinball—bounced from one violent and corrupt trial to another, all because he said that he believed in the resurrection and that God called him to preach to the Gentiles (non-Jews). Now, he's on board a ship that is trying unsuccessfully to sail from the island of Crete (which I've seen from a plane before) due to weather. *Read today's passage.*

Remember this centurion because he's going to come around eventually. Remember that Paul spoke up at the proper time (after the Day of Atonement fast) because he'll speak up again later. We've learned about speaking with proper timing, but have you the boldness to speak up alone like this? Remember, Paul was a *prisoner* on this ship. He knew he would ultimately run out of opportunities to speak.

As my graduation from college approached, I saw my opportunities to lead my friends to Christ rapidly dwindling away. So, one quesadilla lunch date at a time, I spoke up and gave each of them the chance to accept Christ. Are you also like Paul on a ship full of people who need you to speak up? Speak up while you can.

DAY 330

SONG OF SONGS 2:7

Hebrew boys under the age of thirteen were forbidden from reading the Song of Songs (called Song of Solomon in some translations) because it contains intensely sexual poetry. It was almost taken out of the canon of Scripture (the Bible as Protestant [non-Catholic] Christians know it) because it's so graphic. It is a conversation observed among Solomon, his bride, and the bride's friends. I believe this was written before Solomon became a creep and . . . ahem . . . "recruited" several hundred women to keep him company. But if not, from what better man to get advice about women than one who had seven hundred wives and three hundred girlfriends? Ha! *Read today's verse.*

This is the first of three times this charge is given in Song of Songs. It's a call not to mess with sex and love until the time is right. Don't get too hot and heavy with women, my student. Keep things healthy, light, purposeful, and pure. When you're at a stage in your life when you're ready to marry a woman, then it's a different ball game. For now, though, don't repeat the classic mistake of getting overly emotional and overly physical with girls who will turn out not to be your wife!

Day 331

Proverbs 27:18–27

I commend you on how far you have come in reading this book! This easily makes you one of the most studious men your age. Let that marinate for a moment in your heart and think about what that indicates for your future.

Your hard work is going to pay off, if not in the next few years, then in the long run. Trust me. *Read today's text.* Verse 18 is so practical that an atheist could come to the same conclusion. It just makes sense. Now, the work world is not always fair, but hard work does ultimately pay off in the long run.

Don't get bored when you read verses 23–27. It's unlikely that you have lambs and goats, but there's immense wisdom in keeping a record of your resources. These days, we call this a budget. So, remembering to tithe, remembering that your hard work will pay off, and being mindful of your financial goals, write down on the left side of a piece of paper all the money you have coming in this month and on the right side all that you'll be spending. I'm serious about this: write out your budget.

DAY 332

PROVERBS 28:1–8

I have an ambitious prospect for you today. Throughout this book, we have been praying for your Pharisees. Well, now it's time to step out in faith and cash in on those prayers. Go for the jugular. Let's lead your Pharisees to faith in Christ! *Read today's Scripture.*

Be bold as a lion, strong man of God! Evangelize the least likely people to be saved. Evangelize your Pharisees. In case you've forgotten, their names are on the "Praying for These" page at the front of this book. I know it's a bit daunting, but I have personally seen people with alternative lifestyles repent to live Christian lifestyles. I have seen outspoken atheists go into the ministry, and I've even seen a former Satanist become a Christian and then go on a short-term mission trip! It happens! So, go for it. Be bold as a lion (verse 1). Most of those who live their lives far from the gospel do so because they don't actually understand the gospel. So, clear it up for them and watch the Holy Spirit work.

DAY 333

PROVERBS 28:9–18

There are many frustrated people whose prayers go unanswered, and they would do well to learn what you're about to when you read verse 9 of *today's text*.

Those whose prayers are detestable are those who won't even stand to hear what God's Word says. They refuse to hear what God has to say, but expect God to hear what they have to say, perhaps especially when they need something. Detestable indeed.

You can see verse 11 come to fruition today. Just watch a show that has celebrity interviews, and you won't have to wait long. When a celebrity wealthier than you makes some pompous statement that makes you scratch your chin, you're seeing verse 11 realized. Being wealthy does not make one wise, and being wise does not necessarily make you wealthy. Speaking of wisdom, I want you to think hard about verse 13. Are you concealing something today? As we read in James 5:16 and as we see in Ephesians 4, it is better to set aside falsehood and be completely real with your accountability partner(s) than to cover your tracks. Mercy or sin sabotage: the choice is yours. Choose authenticity and experience mercy and freedom.

Day 334

Acts 27:20-32

Back to Paul as he is a prisoner aboard a storm-tossed ship, he is about to get an "I told you so" moment when he turns out to have been absolutely right (verse 21). However, he uses it to deliver this powerful, rousing call to take courage. *Read today's text.*

Are you like the ship in verse 20 right now? Are there no clear signs by which to navigate? Take courage, strong young man of God. Paul timed his first word of caution perfectly and then seems to have remained silent until this moment when it's clear that he was right. Because of his silence as his prediction turned out to be correct, they practically owe it to him to hear him out now. Take note of his excellent use of silence.

He shares this mind-blowing prophecy of good news complete with *two* "take courage" exhortations. He catches two sailors trying to flee. When he takes the prophecy a step further, they take a step of faith and believe Paul. They cut away their lifeboat instead of trying to sneak away in it. Cut away your lifeboat and brave the storm as God has called you. Cut away your backup plan.

Day 335

Acts 27:33–44

*R*ead today's Scripture. Paul has gone from being a lowly prisoner on this massive ship to wielding more influence over its 276 passengers than the ship's captain! I know that the Roman centurion has been *tasked* with guarding Paul, but I wonder how much of the centurion's desire to protect Paul from the soldiers in verses 42 and 43 comes from a sense of respect for Paul and perhaps even belief in Paul's God. Paul has, after all, proven to be right every time.

God spared every person on the ship just as the angel told Paul He would. If you've been under the impression that this vague idea of "God's will" always means prosperity, sweet mushy feelings, and barbecue pulled-pork sandwiches, then take a look at what has just happened to Paul. Remember this: it's sometimes God's will that the ship run aground where He wants it to. *It's sometimes God's will that you be put in harm's way.* God may let your ship be destroyed, but He will spare you.

Day 336

Acts 28:1–6

Read today's Scripture. Again, Paul is definitely doing God's will, and he is definitely in harm's way! The islanders worshipped the goddess Justice and adapted the incomplete view that bad things happen only to people who do bad things. As you know, people who do *good* things suffer too. Paul was serving as Jesus did, helping to feed the fire, when he was bitten! Once again here, nonbelievers were faced with miraculous proof of God, but still did not believe. Now, did you notice the way he just flicked the snake away? That's because he believed God's promise that he would see Rome. May you react the same way when you're "bitten." Resolve now that you'll not freak out and doubt God's promises.

I know why my son died. He died so that people would be reconciled to God, and that sense of purpose brings incredible healing to my grief. That's why I share about Aiden even though it's painful when I do. Remember that, like Paul, you're being watched by nonbelievers in the midst of your trials. Use your trial to point people to Christ, and then you'll know exactly *why* the trial happened to you.

Proverbs 28:19–28

Take a look at your motives and why you might hope to be wealthy one day. *Read today's passage.*

Verse 19 basically says to get real and do what is going to earn a living. Combined with verse 20, the message is to be *faithful* in your work whatever it is, and you will be blessed, but shortcuts don't work. If you stay out of debt, tithe, and save, even a minimum-wage salary for faithful work will earn you *plenty* of money. Don't be greedy (verse 22), but trust in the Lord and you will prosper (verse 25).

Now, *why* prosper at all? Is it just to spend your wealth all on fleeting pleasures (James 4:3)? Is it to outpace other people in your life? God will not bless these, my student. Instead, let your ambition and desire to be successful be driven by your hope to give generously to the kingdom of God! In fact, verse 27 shows that you will never be needy if you give to the poor, but ignoring the poor brings many curses! If you aspire to be wealthy, let it be because you aspire to bless others. God will bless that if it's His will.

PROVERBS 29:1–7

*R*ead today's Scripture. One night, as the guys in my old college ministry got together to study purity from Ephesians 5, the one guy who had gotten married while he was still a student like us opened up about his past struggle with pornography addiction and how he had spent a fortune on it. After counseling helped him experience some victory over pornography, he met his wife. He joked, "Not only is intimacy in marriage better than pornography ever was to me; it's *free* too!" (See verse 3.)

God worked through the wealthy King Solomon's heart to teach us to care for the poor. Verse 7 is a unique thought among Proverbs' many references to the poor because it focuses on the righteous man's awareness of the poor man's *rights*. Let both the destitute and the wealthy have the same *right* to earn your respect. Though you may stand to gain more from befriending wealthy people, show no favoritism. Respect is, I have seen, the most crushing loss to a man who has financially hit rock bottom. So, the next time you do homeless ministry, look the man in the eye. Matthew 25:40 says that in doing this, you honor Jesus.

Day 339

Proverbs 29:8–11

Each man has his own way of dealing with anger. The fool in verse 11 immediately flies off the handle and says everything he wants to say without caring about what happens afterward. He gives full vent to his anger. Other men respond in anger in a more sneaky, subtle, and toxic way. They pack their fury down deep and pretend it's not there until one day it *erupts* like a volcano and destroys everything and the feelings of everyone around it. A better way to deal with anger is to channel it into physical energy and exercise as you cool your head and think about the situation without emotion clouding your perspective on things.

Again, remember that Jesus is our ultimate example for masculinity because of His self-sacrifice. Mark 3:5 gives this awesome account of how Jesus *healed* someone in His anger! Wow! Let your anger bring about healing. Remember that anger in itself is not a sin. In fact, there is a problem with Christian men *not* being angry enough with injustice. Deal with the source of your anger before the day's end (Ephesians 4:26), keep your cool (verse 11), and don't sin in the process (Ephesians 4:26).

DAY 340

ACTS 28:30–31
(The last verses of Acts!)

Read this entire riveting true story that is the book of Acts. I promise you, *your* own church could trace its roots to the events of this book of the Bible! Paul has finally made it to Rome and is doing what he does best. *Read today's Scripture.*

Even when your professors and teachers try to suppress it, proclaim the kingdom of God. Even when you're the only one on the team who believes it, proclaim the kingdom. Even if it costs you everything, proclaim the kingdom of God and do so just as verse 31 says: "with all boldness and without hindrance"! Give yourself a reminder of some sort, whether it's by writing "with all boldness and without hindrance" on your hand or by putting those words as the background on your phone's screen. This way, if you're ever tempted to water down your boldness and be hindered by your fears or what others think, you'll remember! You, strong man of God, are not of "those who draw back and are destroyed, but those who have faith and are saved" (Hebrews 10:39)!

DAY 341

ROMANS 8:18–30

(Let's get familiar with soteriology and then put it to use.)

It's about to get heavy as we look at Romans 8–12. These chapters and the topics they bring up have stirred a discussion among Christians that is as old as the church itself. I'll try to keep from plugging my own take on the Calvinism/Molinism/Arminianism thing and just give you a tour of the text so that you can not only be knowledgeable of the discussion, but put these beautiful truths into action. Calvinists believe that God chooses who is saved, Arminians believe that man alone decides to be saved, and Molinists are in the middle. *Read today's text.*

Verses 29 and 30 bring up something important about God, and that is the fact that He foreknew (knew ahead of time) who would believe and decided before we existed that those who believe would be glorified and made like Jesus when they go to heaven. I know that's heavy, so read these verses again, as they are a big part of the discussion in soteriology (the study of how people are saved). It's okay if you don't totally understand yet. Just know that, though not all things are good, God can make good things come from our troubles (verses 18 and 28).

DAY 342

ROMANS 9:6–21

God chose Israel over all the other nations of the world in the Old Testament days to be the foundation for how people are saved and to show the world how good it is to belong to God. The bottom line is that God is *in charge*. He has the right to show mercy to Jacob, whose name became Israel in Genesis 32:28 and who started the nation of Israel, but not to his twin brother, Esau, who started the nation of Edom. He has the right to harden Pharaoh's heart just as He did in the plagues to bring about the exodus (the Hebrew people leaving Egypt) and show that He was greater than the Egyptian "gods." He alone is God. *Read today's Scripture.*

Verses 11 and 16 lay out that God's choosing Jacob over Esau had nothing to do with Jacob's actions, but with God's merciful covenant with Jacob (which was built upon God's covenant with Abraham). Today we can take part in that covenant that God made in choosing Jacob even if we aren't descended from Jacob (verses 6–8). How is that possible? Through *belief* in Jesus, who is the grand finale of that covenant!

DAY 343

ROMANS 10:1–13

Read today's Scripture. Since Jesus resurrected, everyone who believes in Jesus' resurrection and surrenders in a declaration that Jesus is Lord will be saved (verse 9). That angered the Jews, who didn't like the idea of Gentiles being just as all right before God as they were. It angered them because they had given their whole lives to the old-school way of being all right with God, and that was by obeying all the Old Testament laws. Thankfully, today it's not about sticking to laws, but about faith in Jesus (verse 4)!

Verse 9 is the most straightforward verse in the Bible about how to be saved because it starts with "If" and ends with "you will be saved." If you're confused by all this soteriology stuff, it's okay: just get verse 9. I use it *constantly* to explain to people how to be saved. Verse 13 might sound familiar because it's quoting the same verse from Joel 2 that Peter quoted in his message in Acts 2 that jump-started the church. "Everyone who calls on the name of the Lord will be saved" (verse 13). Yep, that means *everyone*—even the most lost person you know.

DAY 344

ROMANS 11:7–17

Romans 9 teaches about God's covenant choosing of Israel. Romans 10 elaborates on the idea that it's not only those who are descendants of Israel who can be saved (Romans 9:6–8), but *everyone* who calls upon Jesus' name (Romans 10:9, 13). *Read today's passage.*

So, the Jews who rejected Christ (Romans 9:1–5) are hardened just as Pharaoh was hardened (Romans 11:7–8), but God is not giving up on His chosen people (Revelation 7:4–8), who descended from Abraham, Isaac, and Jacob (Romans 11:28).

The imagery here is one of a vine that represents chosen Israel, and on that vine God attaches new branches that represent Gentiles (non-Jews) who believe. So, in chapter 11, we see God's sovereign right to choose (chapter 9) working in a beautiful balance with man's freedom to believe (chapter 10).

Calvinism, which may also refer to "reformed theology," is summarized by the five points of Calvinism, and Romans 9 is a major chapter in this soteriology. Arminianism is summarized by the Five Articles of Remonstrance, and Romans 10 is more its style. There's plenty of middle ground between these two soteriologies (like Molinism), and wherever you choose to set up your tent, make sure you keep *all* of Scripture in mind.

DAY 345

ROMANS 12:1–2
(So-what-eriology?)

Let's start out by worshipping with the song "Your Love Never Fails" by the worship band Jesus Culture. We've read Romans 8:28, which is quoted in the song's lyrics, and we've read about God's unfailing love as He finished what He started in His covenant with Jacob. In the decades I've walked with Christ, His love has *never* failed me, so sing to Him now. Then *read today's text.*

Did you catch that "therefore"? Having surveyed Romans 8–11, you know what it's there for. All of this heady theology stuff ends in something practical. These two verses tell us how to figure out God's specific will. We present ourselves to God in worship like we just did at the start of today's devotional, and we don't conform to the world's mind-set. Then, in this worshipful state, consecrated before God in preparation for what He's going to do through us (Joshua 3:5), we can discern (figure out) God's will. Trying to figure out a big question about your future? Start with worship. It's easier to see God's will from a worshipful state. It's dangerous to try to discern God's will in a state of rebellion against God.

Day 346

Proverbs 29:12–17

Ahhh . . . After a long trip away, we're back home in Proverbs, the book of wisdom for young men. *Read today's Scripture.*

Let's talk leadership. You may not be in an official place of leadership or even feel that you are particularly called to be a leader, but walking an upright life in full view of non-Christians *is* a form of leadership, so these principles apply to you as well. Verse 13 makes me think of God's perspective on a poor leader who is oppressive. As leaders, we must take into consideration the fact that, though we have power over others, God is the ultimate power over us, and we must give an account to Him for how we lead. Part of this is choosing wisely those to whom you listen (verse 12). Don't be an oppressor: be an inspirer. Be the kind of leader people *want* to follow. Act in such a way that makes your followers proud to be counted among your ranks.

DAY 347

PROVERBS 29:18

Read today's verse. Translations vary considerably here, but the idea is that people need a vision from their leadership. Otherwise, things go into chaos. Craig Groeschel writes about this in his book *It,* comparing it to a scene that unfolded at a dog-racing track. The dogs usually chase this mechanical "rabbit" as it runs along a rail inside the track. At one race, the doors opened, the dogs shot out, the bunny took off . . . and then suddenly exploded. The dogs no longer had a clear thing to chase after, and chaos ensued. Dogs stopped running, meandered around the track, howled at the people in the stands, and not one dog finished the race.

Building on the leadership principles we saw yesterday, you as a leader and man of God need a clear sense of vision and purpose. If you don't know where you're going, it's unnerving for the people who follow you. The people on your team are not dumb. They can sense a lack of vision, and you can bet that *someone* is going to lead even if they have to break ranks to do it. The person with the most influence is the true leader, and men of vision have the greatest influence.

DAY 348

PROVERBS 29:19–27

Let's start today with a checkup. As we begin to close out our walk together through this book, I want you to think back on where we started. Review your "Praying for These" page. Seriously, celebrate the victories God has brought about especially when it comes to people being saved, like your Andrew and Philip, and the fruit of their ministry, Peter. Praise God if you saw Nicodemus come around because *you* are blessed by that. Also, I say we finish this 365 devotional series out in an all-out sprint when it comes to evangelizing the Pharisees in your life. Go big! Evangelize as if God's on your side . . . because He is!

Read today's text. Verses 19 and 24 show the foolishness of knowing what we ought to do, but still doing what we shouldn't. As Jesus said to the Pharisees, the fact that you aren't blind to God's law is part of what makes you guilty of sin. Such stubbornness is rooted in pride and, as verse 23 reminds us, God humbles the proud and honors the humble. So, today simply abide by what you know you ought to do and do so from a humble heart.

Day 349

Revelation 1:1–20

(Our last series will be a survey of the last book of the Bible.)

Men must rise to face challenges. Like a video game, the content of our devotionals has become increasingly difficult. You made it through that series on soteriology in Romans; now let's step it up and hit Revelation. *Read today's Scripture.* According to verse 3, you are blessed if you read the book of Revelation. Cool, huh? Good luck, though, because this is *the* hardest book of the Bible to understand. So, we reunite with John, the one whose Gospel we read, after the Romans exiled him to this tiny island called Patmos. There, God showed him how the days of this earth as we know it will end. It begins with this letter to the churches, which are represented by lampstands. Jesus walks among them (verse 13) just as He does our churches today. The first letter is to the Ephesian church, and I recommend reading that one sometime.

Close today by reading verses 12–16 and imagining Jesus as He is described. Hear His roaring waterfall-like voice, and let this be an act of worship as you do.

DAY 350

REVELATION 4:1–11

Read today's text. The sheer awesome power described in the throne room of heaven helps me to understand why it is that we cannot see God. As God told Moses on Mount Sinai, no one can see God and live. His power and holiness are just too great for us as sinful men, so He conceals Himself from our sight partially for our own protection. Look at John's reaction back in Revelation 1:17 after the resurrected Jesus spoke to him; he fell down at Jesus' feet "like a dead man." Even these twenty-four elders of heaven fall down and worship God (Revelation 5:14). Angels like the seraphim described in Isaiah 6 day and night never stop saying, "Holy, holy, holy, Lord God, the Almighty, who was, who is, and who is to come" (verse 8). How remarkable that Isaiah wrote his prophecy several centuries before John, yet the two men describe the same scene.

Today's challenge is truly amazing because you are about to join in with these angels and elders in their worship. Worship God with "Revelation Song" written by Jennie Lee Riddle, and sing *with* those angels to the almighty God who *is* returning one amazing day!

DAY 351

REVELATION 5:1–7

John falls into despair because a scroll containing what I interpret to be the glory of God and the ransom for mankind cannot be opened. *Read today's passage.*

Referring to Jesus as the Lamb in Revelation has its roots in the Old Covenant. The Bible is so beautifully comprehensive. In the final plague before the exodus, the blood of a lamb on a family's doorpost is what spared them the death of their firstborn son. In the Old Covenant, the family's pet lamb would be slain at the altar as an offering to God to atone for (pay for) sin. Imagine the shock of seeing the lamb's blood and thinking, *This lamb did nothing wrong, but I am guilty of sin.* Every lamb sacrificed, especially those from the first Passover, was a foretelling of the ultimate Lamb, and that's Jesus. In fact, Jesus transformed the Passover meal into what we call the Lord's Supper today by saying that the wine symbolized *His* blood. Again, imagine the shock of seeing *that* Lamb's blood knowing that He suffers for the wrong *you* have done. This is why Jesus is called the Lamb. This is why *He* is worthy to open the scroll.

Day 352

Proverbs 30:1–10

We've finished the Proverbs of Solomon, and now we hear from God through a dude named Agur. These final two chapters of Proverbs, as you'll see, have a totally different style and feel from their predecessors. God again sovereignly works through our system to align adjacent devotionals so that, though they are from different texts written millennia apart, they appear side by side in this devotional to teach the same concepts together and prove the cohesiveness (togetherness) of the Bible. *Read today's text.*

Verse 4 reminds me of this awesome section in the book of Job wherein God puts Job in his place. Verse 6 is strikingly similar to a verse we're coming up on in Revelation that warns us not to add to or take away from the Bible.

Verses 7–9 give a sense of balance to Proverbs because Solomon was richer than an NFL player's ex-wife, and these verses show how good it is to have simply enough. Pray a promise to God that you will never, if you become wealthy, forget Him (verse 9).

DAY 353

PROVERBS 30:11–23

Agur, the earthly author of this Proverb, structures these funny verses according to number games. They may seem odd, but they teach unique lessons in cool ways. *Today's text* is going to be different from any proverb you've ever read.

Honor your father or father figure today, and if she's around, do something to bless your mother. Do something to help your dad, and buy your mom a thoughtful gift in light of verses 11 and 17. This is your challenge for the day.

The overarching theme of these verses is gluttonous dissatisfaction, and it applies brilliantly to lust. Beware the slippery slope of pornography and messing around in lust (verse 19). You'll never reach a point at which you can sit back and say, "I'm satisfied." Instead, sexual actions outside of marriage leave you craving more each time, and they eat you alive spiritually as they do (verse 20).

Take hope today when you think about the long marathon to marriage if that's God's will for you. Though sex in marriage will take your whole life to perfect, there's immense satisfaction to be had in it, and that satisfaction is not tainted with sin. No, it ends in a full heart.

DAY 354

PROVERBS 30:24–33

Before writing this, I prayed for your accountability group and for your relationships with wise, godly men. Know that you are prayed for today.

I was on mission in Kenya, teaching a student camp, drumming for some churches, and ministering to orphans when I first heard a hyrax. A hyrax is like a small beaver with a tiny tail. One night as I walked from one of our cabins to the other, I took a "pit stop" under an acacia tree that was halfway up the trail. As I began to empty my "tank," I heard from directly above me this incredibly loud and indescribable sound. It didn't take me long to finish after that. You have to look up a recording of the sound. I mention it because *today's text* talks about the hyrax.

These cautions against pride that pop up all over the book of Proverbs are like warning signs on a road that's heading off a cliff. By this time, having seen this warning sign so often, I hope you see how increasingly dangerous it will be for you to exalt yourself. The fact that you're reading this means you can't say you weren't warned!

DAY 355

LAMENTATIONS 3:22–24

One of my students told me about what he thought was a new song by Third Day called "Your Love, Oh Lord" which is based on Psalm 57:10 and 108:4. In a microsecond, my mind was flooded with memories of my devotional times in this old, broken-in chair. The song actually came out when I was a freshman in high school, and I used to sing it to God from my knees in my bedroom. I didn't have a degree and didn't know much about the Bible. I just passionately *loved Jesus*. I've been through so much since then, and God has remained *faithful* through it all. Today I can worship God with a truly deep, tested, and proven appreciation for God's faithfulness. He has never failed me, though I've failed Him. *Read today's Scripture.*

This is one of fourteen alphabetically arranged Bible passages. Those funny characters that top each section are the Hebrew alphabet, and each section would have started (from the *right*) with its corresponding Hebrew letter. Read today's text and then sing "Your Love, Oh Lord" or "Your Love Never Fails." Thank God for all that He has done in your journey through this book.

DAY 356

REVELATION 6:1–14

The seals that only Jesus the Lamb can open will set off an outline of events. Here's a twenty-five-dollar word: *eschatology*. It refers to the study of the end times. Your eschatological view is your interpretation of the order in which the events of Revelation take place and their nature. Some eschatological views include premillennialism, amillennialism, dispensationalism, covenant theology, the pre-tribulation view, and the post-tribulation view. Pick your flavor. Here come the four horsemen of the apocalypse in today's text!

We'll see this rider on the white horse return because he is the antichrist. However, you won't see the word *antichrist* in Revelation. Instead, he's called "the beast." The sense of peace that the antichrist first horseman brings is false and gives way to the war of the second horse, the complete economic collapse of the third, and Death, who rides the fourth. The fifth seal is about Christian martyrs (people who die for their beliefs) like Stephen, whose death we studied in Acts 7. The sixth seal is the big show: the day of God's wrath. The wrath of God is fierce and good. It's fierce because God hates evil. It's good because evil gets its tail kicked!

Day 357

Revelation 9:1–12

Do you feel as if you've reached the boss level of a video game by finishing this book and reading this heavy stuff from Revelation? You should, bro. At this point, things on earth are getting *crazy,* with mass suffering and even a huge, flaming star crashing into earth and poisoning its water (Revelation 8:10–11). Crack your knuckles and *read today's text.*

Why all of this suffering? Why do all of these crazy things happen particularly to those who don't have God's seal on their foreheads (verse 4)? I believe it is so that these events would be unmistakably accredited to the Bible by those who have been denying the Bible, those who suffer for five months from one of these locust stings and other woes. You see, people who have not heard the gospel will be able to come to Christ even after the rapture, when all believers are brought to be with Christ in the air. Those who remain afterward and still refuse to make the obvious (literally *painfully* obvious) connection between what will be happening in the world and these detailed prophecies *must* be extremely hard-hearted. So, these drastic measures are what it takes to reach such drastically lost hearts.

DAY 358

REVELATION 11:7–14

Here's one of Revelation's most fascinating prophecies. God sends these two supernaturally powerful men to serve as His witnesses in the days of the antichrist. They proclaim the gospel constantly for 1,260 days (remember that's about 3.5 years) and defend themselves with fire from their mouths! They can stop the rain, turn water into blood old-school-style, and have been given the freedom by God to bring absolutely *any* plague they want upon the earth *whenever* they want (Revelation 11:1–6). These guys are cooler than Shark Week! Remembering that the beast is the antichrist and paying attention to the numbers, *read today's Scripture*.

These men are described in verse 4 as olive trees (symbols of peace) and lampstands (things that give light) because God is making the gospel *undeniably* obvious to the world before they're killed. Verse 9, describing how the world will see their dead bodies, used to be a topic of ridicule against Christianity . . . until television was invented, making that completely possible. They preached for 3.5 years and resurrected after 3.5 days, going to heaven on a cloud. Though seven thousand *ridiculously* hard-hearted people die in an earthquake, God will still save many people through it all in verse 13.

DAY 359

EZEKIEL 37:1–14

This way back to when we studied apologetics. Do you remember seeing the revival of Israel as a nation in 1948 prophesied in the Bible thousands of years before it happened? *Read today's passage.*

It's possible that Ezekiel saw the skeletal remains found in concentration camps after the Holocaust. After World War II, Jewish people displaced by the Holocaust found themselves relocated to the exact same plot of land that was once called Israel two thousand long years prior. Israel became a nation again all at once with its own government, currency, military, and everything (Isaiah 66:8–9). The next day, the countries surrounding Israel all declared war on Israel. Israel defeated every one of them and still exists today.

Those dry bones rising to become a vast, unconquerable army first refer to Israel coming back and kicking tail, but I think that God wants to do this in the church as well. Let the revival that has taken place in your heart spread to others so that the dead church would *rise up and become a vast army of evangelism!* Let those with once dead faith arise and break the silence. Pray for this now.

DAY 360

PROVERBS 31:1–3

It's time to read the letter you wrote to yourself at the start of this book! Go to the introduction and read the blank you filled in with the letter's location.

I hope that, since you have crossed the raging Jordan River that is this book, you'll look back to the far shore from whence you started this journey. In the best sense possible, I hope that you do not recognize the younger man on the other side looking back at you through this letter. If you are disappointed, I don't want you to be disheartened. Instead, *bow up* and make happen in the next five days everything you have not yet fulfilled in your letter's description!

Read today's text. King Lemuel now writes to his son, and his letter is very kingly-focused, but we non-royal men can still benefit from it. Verse 3 brings to mind the energy that is wasted in lustful acts. Let yourself mourn a bit right now over the loss of what could have been if you had used that energy on godly things. If you've fallen short of your letter's expectations, how much of that is due to energy wasted on lust?

DAY 361

PROVERBS 31:4-7

*R*ead today's text. You've now read all of what Proverbs has to say about alcohol and as such can now make a biblically informed decision about where you'll stand when you are of age. This text makes a compelling case to be a teetotaler (someone who does not drink at all), though it is not a command. Verses 6 and 7 show alcohol's purpose. This recommendation cannot be given on biblical authority, but only on my personal experience: I recommend that you remain a teetotaler at least through college. I did it, and *it helped me keep my virginity until marriage*. It also opened up some great witnessing opportunities because you stand out in a good way. *Also, being the only sober person at a party full of drunk people is like being a superhero!* Many college students overdo it and shipwreck their expensive educations, but *not you*, my student.

You need to begin working out your convictions before the world shapes your convictions for you. Romans 14 teaches that you need to be *considerate*, *sure*, and *private* about your stance (Romans 14:21–23). Make a decision.

DAY 362

PROVERBS 31:8-9

Slavery still exists today. Did you know that? Abortion kills a *completely* innocent unborn child every second worldwide. Christian missionaries continue to be martyred (remember the fifth seal in Revelation?) around the world. These people are unable to speak up for themselves, but you have a voice. With this unjust suffering in mind, *read today's Scripture.*

Twice, our Bible instructs us to speak up! As we've established, the Bible needs only give such a call or command once for it to be God's truth, and here we are exhorted *twice*. If you're into social media, post something today to speak up for those who have no voice (verse 8). Also, consider doing something incredibly bold and standing up on a table to shout it. When you speak up, do so in the way that is most likely to raise awareness effectively, and that is by *not* speaking down to people, making them feel guilty for something that is not their fault, or by making yourself the focus. Instead, speak to them as you would if you were the quarterback and they were your offensive huddle. If you don't know what to say, then just share these two beautiful verses!

Day 363

Proverbs 31:10–31

(Today, we finish the one book that has been with us the whole way!)

Even if you and I have never met, I have reason to believe that you are a man worthy of masculine affirmation because *you are finishing what you started! You are a man!* The fact that you are reading this right now indicates that you are doing well in the indefinitely long period of preparation for marriage. So, as we finish Proverbs, we get a glimpse at and pray for your future bride! *Read today's Scripture.*

May your future bride's beauty be her fear of the Lord (verse 30)! As we studied in the beginning, Jesus is the ultimate example of masculinity because Jesus lived out the most masculine thing a man could do: self-sacrifice. So, you are going to, as we said on Day 1, do likewise to an extent. I want you to fast for twenty-four hours starting now. Let your convictions dictate *how* you'll fast (drink only water, etc.). Every time your empty stomach burns, I want you to pray for your future wife. Plan to break your fast right before tomorrow's record-length devotional. As you fast, write your future wife a letter, and keep it in this book as a gift for her, whoever she is!

Day 364

Revelation 21:1–27

(This passage is long, so plan your devotional time well.)

Did you just *feast* like a starving killer whale that jumped the wall into the penguin exhibit? I hope so . . . though I hope no children were watching. *Read today's Scripture.*

I cannot wait to meet my Savior. Like the original recipients of 1 Peter who were under the persecution of Nero, I put my hope in heaven. But there is something else about heaven that makes me even more excited: I get to see my son Aiden again. What will he say to me? "Dad" would be enough. I'm going to give my boy such a violent hug. Even writing this, my chest aches to feel him against me. I want to bring as many people as I can to this *awesome* place that is illuminated not by some mere G2 dwarf star like our sun, but by the *direct presence of God!*

That day is coming when Satan is *defeated* (Revelation 20:10), and God will wipe away every tear, and death will be no more! If you understand this passage, then like the friends of the paralyzed man in Mark 2, you will stop at *nothing* to bring your friends to Jesus! Be as relentless as heaven is glorious! Go!

DAY 365

REVELATION 22:16–21

So, our time together through this book comes to a close with the very last verses of the Bible! *Read our final text!*

Earlier we learned that this Bible of yours is Jesus in Word form, and that He existed as this perfect Word before the foundations of the earth. Here, Jesus Himself addresses us through John at the Bible's end.

What is the final message of the Bible? *Jesus is coming back!* Verse 20 is the prayer of the church, which is the bride of Christ, calling Jesus to come back: "Amen! Come, Lord Jesus!" This used to make me pause. I thought, *God, I have so much that I want to* do *before You come back.* Then, in studying Peter's life and the time that he is rebuked by Jesus in Matthew 16:23, I came to see that my apprehension was a desire for God's will *not* to be realized, and so I repented. Do not close this book until you can be so surrendered to the will of God that you can, in absolute honesty before God, pray, "Amen! Come, Lord Jesus!"

I am so proud of you, strong man of God.

SUBJECT GUIDE

The numbers listed indicate the devotional day.